Practical Forging and Art Smithing

GW01066333

Thomas F. Googerty

Alpha Editions

This edition published in 2024

ISBN 9789361476259

Design and Setting By

Alpha Editions

www.alphaedis.com

Email - info@alphaedis.com

Contents

INTRODUCTION

The present demand for school instruction in the industrial arts has made it necessary for the teachers of industries to have that knowledge of materials and methods which can only result from long and careful experience with the materials of industry.

This book is the result of a life of such experience by a man who is now recognized as a master craftsman in wrought metal.

The author's work in wrought iron is comparable in design and finish to the best work that has been produced in that material.

Some pieces of the best German work are before me as I make this statement and tho more intricate they are no better in execution and far less suitable to the material in design than the pieces illustrated in this book which I have seen in process of execution and in the finished form.

The author has moreover been a teacher of wrought metal work for many years.

This experience is reflected in the sequence of difficulty presented by the exercises and the clear, simple statement of the text.

With such clear and exact statement and with such profuse illustration it is evident that the metal worker can gather much of the author's long experience from this book and take many a short cut to success in an accomplishment to which there can be no royal road.

But the effectiveness of an applied art is measured best by its expression of purpose within the limitations of the material used.

The artistic success of this book lies in the evident fact that the work represented appears "Hand wrought and fashioned to beauty and use."

I predict for it increasing usefulness in setting right the practice of forging in school shops and as an inspiration to teachers, craftsmen and tradesmen.

EDWARD J. LAKE.

CHAPTER I.

The Forge—Forge Tools—The Anvil—Anvil Tools—Making the Fire—Cleaning the Fire—Welding—Flux and Its Uses.

One of the most essential things in the school forge shop is a good forge and fire; half the work is then mastered. A few years ago nearly all of the small commercial shops running from one to six or more fires were equipped with brick or iron forges. The blast was furnished either with a bellows or fan which had to be turned by hand. This method was a great drawback, which resulted in much loss of time. It was impossible to do much work without the aid of a helper. Work that required two men in those days is being done now by one. Modern invention has played an important part in simplifying the labors of the workers in iron and steel. At the present time there are various kinds of forges in use that lessen the work of the smith. The most successful factories are now equipped with modern forges and appliances in order that they may be able to do work quickly.

In our manual training schools, where the pupils have such short periods in which to do work, it is necessary that the shops be equipped with modern tools so that they can produce work quickly. This will give the individual pupil more practice in a shorter length of time, which simply means more knowledge. Our schools should not be hampered by using forges that have been out-of-date for years.

The best forge for manual training and trade schools is the down draft with power driven fans, thus eliminating all pipes overhead and doing away with the dust and dirt. A boy, working at this kind of a forge, can use both hands in the handling of the work being heated in the fire; this is a great advantage over the old way of turning a crank. Another good feature of the mechanical draft forge is that it teaches a boy early how to avoid over-heating or burning his iron. This is the first thing one must learn in working at forging, as one who cannot heat the metal properly cannot work it. One must become acquainted with the material, and the burning heat must be understood.

Fig. 1. A Typical School Forge.

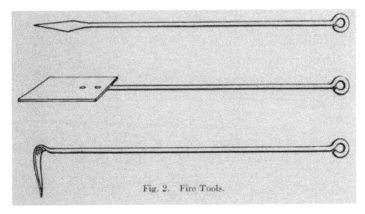

Fig. 2. Fire Tools.

Figure 1 shows an illustration of a down draft forge suitable for schools; it is made of cast iron. A pressure fan furnishes the blast for the fire and an exhaust fan takes away the gas and smoke thru an opening at the bottom of the hood, and thru a large pipe which continues under the floor and out thru a flue. The hood represented at A, can be moved backward and forward to catch the smoke. The hood is moved with a crank and worm gear as shown at B. The hearth is shown at C; a hole in the center is called the tuyere. This is where the fire is built and is the outlet for the wind. The amount of air needed for the fire is regulated by a valve that is moved with a rod shown at D. The coal box is always at the right hand of any forge and is shown at E. The water box is represented at F. At G is shown the pressure pipe and at H the exhaust pipe. Notice the large opening under the forge at I. Thru this opening any nut or screw under the tuyere can be tightened with ease. Notice the slide-rod at J. This rod, when pulled, dumps the cinders out of the tuyere, and a bucket may be set under the hearth to catch them. In school shops these forges are generally set in pairs in order to save room. Figure 2 shows three fire-tools needed for the forge fire. These tools consist of a poker made from $\frac{3}{8}$-inch round stock, 26 inches long with a loose eye turned on one end for a handle; a shovel with a flat blade 4 by 6 by $\frac{1}{16}$ inches with a handle riveted to the blade, and a tool called a scraper. This scraper is made from the same stock as the poker and is made with an eye at one end and a flat hook at the other. It is used to scrape the coal and coke onto the fire, and to move pieces of coke or coal, so that the iron may be seen while heating.

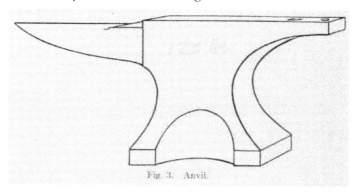

Fig. 3. Anvil.

The anvil should be of wrought iron with a steel face, weighing about 125 pounds. This is large enough for any work being done in manual training schools. In the school shop the anvils should all be of the same size and weight so that any tool used with them will fit into any square hole. In factories where anvils are made, they are forged from wrought iron or soft steel, with a carbon steel face welded on; some are cast steel thruout and others are cast iron with a steel face. The face is generally three-quarters inch thick, and is hardened to resist heavy blows from the hammer and sledge. (See drawing Figure 3 of anvil.) The anvil should be fastened with iron straps, on a 10 by 10-inch block, set into the ground about $3\frac{1}{2}$ feet. From the top of the anvil to the floor should measure 26 inches. The proper place to set the anvil in relation to the forge is shown in the drawing, Figure 4. The smith should stand between the forge and the anvil, with the horn of the anvil at his left when facing it. The anvil edge farthest from the smith is called the outer edge and the one nearest the smith is called the inner edge.

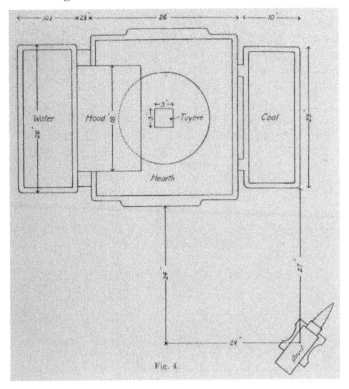

Fig. 4.

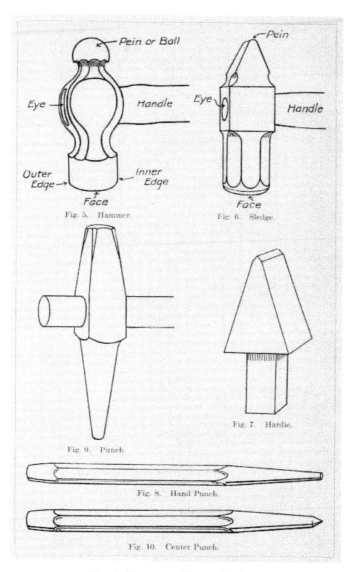

Fig. 5. Hammer. Fig. 6. Sledge.

Fig. 9. Punch. Fig. 7. Hardie.

Fig. 8. Hand Punch.

Fig. 10. Center Punch.

Every anvil should have two ball hammers weighing about 1½ and 2 lbs. each. (See drawing of hammer, Figure 5.) The hammers should be numbered corresponding with a number on the anvil. All the hammers should be kept in a rack when not in use. When the pupils come into the shop to work, they should be assigned to a certain forge and held responsible for the care of tools. A ten-pound sledge hammer should also be included, perhaps one for every two forges; the handle should be 26 inches long. (See Figure 6.)

A piece of tool steel fitted into the square hole of the anvil and sharpened at the top, is called a hardie. It is used in cutting iron. A piece of iron is set on the sharpened edge of the hardie and struck with the hammer. The sharpened edge of the hardie cuts into the iron, and in this manner it is cut deep enough so that it may be broken. (See drawing of hardie, Figure 7.)

If a piece of steel is pointed on one end, it can be hammered thru a flat piece of iron. This is one method of punching holes in iron; a steel punch so made is called a hand punch. Ordinarily hand punches are made out of $\frac{1}{2}$-inch to $\frac{3}{4}$-inch hexagonal tool-steel bars about eleven inches long. (See drawing Figure 8.) For heavy punching, a short, thick punch with a hole thru it, (called the eye) to receive a wooden handle, is used. This kind of punch is struck on with a sledge hammer. (See drawing Figure 9.)

A center punch is used to make depressions in metal so that a drill may be started in a given place. It is used also to mark places or distances on the surface of metal when the metal is to be bent at a certain place. Center punches are made from hexagonal tool steel about 4 by $\frac{1}{2}$-inch, drawn to a point and ground to a short angle. (See Figure 10.)

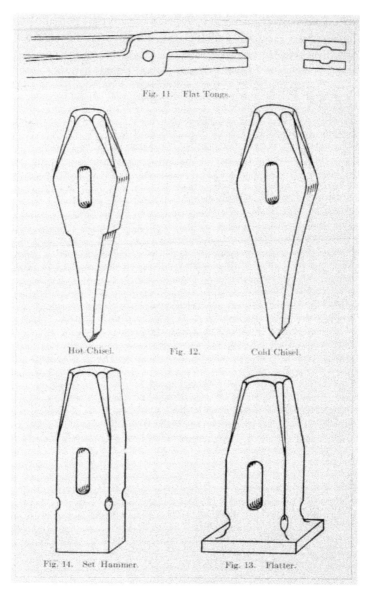

Fig. 11. Flat Tongs.

Fig. 12. Hot Chisel. Cold Chisel.

Fig. 13. Flatter. Fig. 14. Set Hammer.

In heating and handling short pieces of stock, tongs are used (see Figure 11) which are made from Swedish iron or mild steel; they are made in various sizes and shapes according to use. They are called pick-ups, flat, round-nose, and bolt tongs according to the shape of the lips. Tongs should always be made to fit the piece being forged. One cannot hold a piece of iron properly with tongs that do not fit the piece. They may be heated and fitted to the stock when occasion demands. One important reason why tongs should fit the piece being hammered, is that when turning and striking the piece there is danger of the piece being knocked out of the tongs in a whirling motion and the flying piece of hot iron is liable to strike someone; this danger must be closely watched. Tongs should not be heated red hot and cooled in water; this destroys them.

Hot and cold chisels are used in cutting stock. The blade of the hot chisel is made very thin, while the cold chisel is made blunt to stand the heavy strain in cutting. They are generally made with a hole thru them, called the eye, to receive a wooden handle. These chisels are struck on with a sledge hammer. (See Figure 12.)

Iron and steel are sometimes smoothed with a tool called a flatter. This tool is struck on with a sledge, and should not be used to stretch iron. Its purpose is only to give the work a smooth finish. Figure 13 shows a flatter, and Figure 14 a set-hammer. The set-hammer is always used to smooth and draw stock. All of these tools are made from tool-steel.

A heading tool is made from a flat piece of soft steel with a hole in one end. Sometimes a carbon steel face is welded on. The heading tool is used mostly in heading bolts. Heading tools are made with different sized holes. (See Figure 15.)

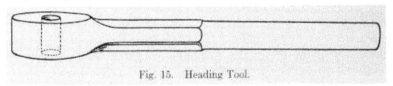
Fig. 15. Heading Tool.

Fig. 15. Heading Tool.

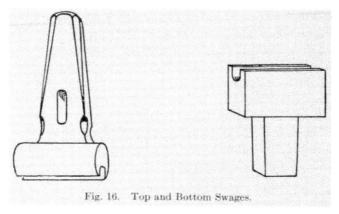

Fig. 16. Top and Bottom Swages.

Fig. 16. Top and Bottom Swages.

Swages and fullers are used to smooth and form iron into various shapes. The swages generally have half round depressions in them. They are made in pairs called top and bottom swage. The bottom one fits the square hole of the anvil; the top one has a hole for a wooden handle. (See drawing Figure 16.) The fullers are also made in pairs called top and bottom fullers. They are used to make depressions in metal. (See drawing Figure 17.) When referring to swages, fullers, and other tools of this character, blacksmiths speak of anvil tools. Special anvil tools are used in doing various kinds of forging, and are made when needed. The anvil tools should be kept in a tool rack next to the anvil. These tools should be made from tool-steel of about 75-point carbon, or they may be purchased from a dealer. Some tools, such as swages, that do not require continuous service, are made of soft steel.

The anvil tool should have a buggy-spoke for a handle. The handle should stick thru the eye of the hole about one inch and should never be wedged. If the handle is wedged it is more liable to be broken when the tool is struck a glancing blow with the sledge hammer. This is very often the case. The reason the spoke should stick thru the tool is that if it should begin to work off the handle when struck with the sledge hammer, the movement can be seen.

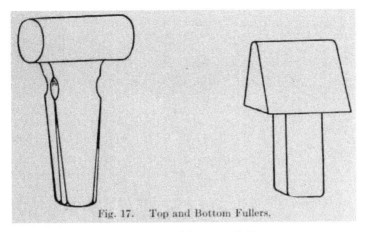

Fig. 17. Top and Bottom Fullers.

Figure 18 shows a wrought vise suitable for school work. A cast iron machinists' vise should not be used excepting, perhaps, for bench work. Figure 19 shows a cast-iron swage block with various sized holes, and depressions around the edge for forming iron.

The stock used in a forge shop should be kept in a rack built for the purpose. The different kinds of stock, such as soft and tool-steel, common and Swedish iron, should be partly painted with a distinguishing color, so that there will be no trouble finding what is wanted. For instance, all soft steel should be painted white, tool-steel another color, and so on. There should also be in the shop a shears to cut iron. One of the ordinary hand-power shears in use today would be suitable and may be purchased from a dealer.

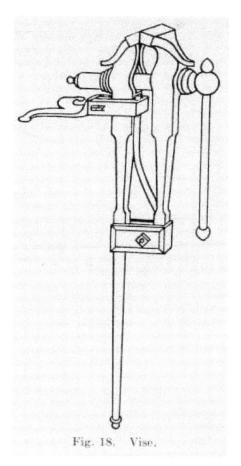

Fig. 18. Vise.

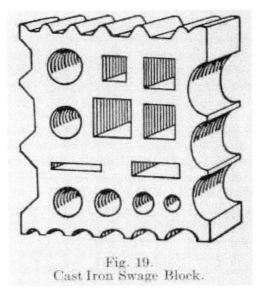

Fig. 19.
Cast Iron Swage Block.

Fig. 19. Cast Iron Swage Block.

In lighting the fire in the forge all of the cinders are cleaned out down to the tuyere. This is done by scraping them to the sides of the fire-place with the shovel. All clinkers should be picked out with the hands and put under the forge. It is a good plan to pick out some of the best pieces of coke and set them to one side on the forge, to be used later on. The slide rod that controls the ash dump at the bottom of the tuyere, is now pulled to allow the cinders and ashes to drop thru. Do not allow a boy to pull the valve after the fire is started, as this wastes the coke and is a bad habit to get into.

When the tuyere is clean, some shavings are lighted in the bottom and when well burned, the coke is raked back on the fire. A little wind is then turned on. Wet coal is banked around the sides and back of the fire. When the fire is well started and loosened up in front with the poker and most of the smoke burned, it is ready for heating. The coal in the box should be thoroly mixed with water before putting it on the fire, for the reason that it cokes better, and packs in around the sides of the fire, keeping it from breaking thru. The coal box is always at the right of the worker when he is facing the fire. The box on his left, and between the down draft forges, is to hold water—not coal. There should be a water cup of some sort hanging on a hook so that when water is needed for fire or coal it may be handled with the cup.

A fire, when not properly handled becomes hollow, due to the center burning out. If iron is heated in this kind of a fire, it will become oxidized, that is to say, a dirty scale will form over the metal. Iron cannot be properly heated, and it is impossible to get the welding heat with a fire in this condition. The reason a fire becomes hollow is that it may be filled with clinkers, or too much blast may have been used, and when it comes in contact with the pieces being heated causes them to cool and oxidize. Sometimes the fire will not be directly over the hole in the tuyere; which is one cause of poor heating. This is a common fault with boys working at the forge. Always have the fire over the hole in the tuyere, and not to one side.

When the fire becomes hollow and dirty, clean it by picking out the clinkers with the poker or scraper, then move the sides of the fire towards the center of the tuyere with the shovel, keeping the well-coked inner sides near the center of the tuyere, and having the center of fire over the hole in the tuyere. Wet coal is now banked around the outer sides. Always have a thick bed of coke under the piece being heated and regulate the blast so as not to burn out the center of the fire at once. See drawing of fire with piece about on the same plane with bottom of hearth; notice dotted lines representing the wrong way to put stock in the fire. (Fig. 20.)

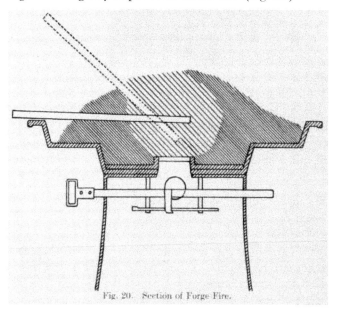

Fig. 20. Section of Forge Fire.

Fig. 20. Section of Forge Fire.

If two pieces of iron are placed in the fire and heated, they will become gradually softer until they reach a state where the metal has become sticky. If touched together the two pieces will stick. This is what is known as welding heat. If they were taken to the anvil and hammered while in this condition they would unite and become one piece. This would be called welding. All metals cannot be welded. Iron, soft steel, low-carbon tool steel and spring steel can be welded.

A flux is used in welding steel—this excludes the air and forms a pasty surface on the metal which is squeezed out from between the surfaces of the metal when hammered. Borax and the many welding compounds are used. Very seldom is it necessary to use a flux on iron. Clean sand, which is good, is used by many. Borax or welding compound is sometimes used on very thin stock. For ordinary welding, such as is being done in school shops, borax should never be used. It is poor practice, unnecessary, and a useless waste.

In heating iron, if it is brought beyond the welding heat, it will become softer and softer until it will finally burn. This may be known by the great number of little explosive sparks coming from the fire. These little sparks are particles of iron separating from the bar and burning. As the heat gradually rises, the metal separates. If the bar were now placed on the anvil and struck a hard blow with a hammer, it would fly to pieces. Therefore, judgment must be used in striking the first blow on any welding heat—it should be light. The succeeding blows should be made gradually harder. A hard blow at the start might make the metal fly to pieces, or make the upper piece slip away from the under piece. If lighter blows were struck, the weld might be made in good shape.

The principal thing in welding is to have a clean fire. All of the clinkers must be kept out. The fire should be a well burned one, without much smoke or gas, and never any green coal near the pieces being heated. Well burned pieces of coke around the metal should always be used in raising the welding heat. In raising the welding heat very little blast should be used at first. Heat the pieces slowly so as to get them hot thruout.

CHAPTER II.

Electric Welding—Oxy-acetylene Gas Welding—The Fagot Weld—
The Separate Heat Weld—Scarfing—Upsetting—Making the
Weld—Lap Welding Without Scarfing—Jump Welding—Butt
Weld—Split Welding—Corner Weld—T Weld.

A rapid blast on the start, not only heats the outer part of the metal first and not the center, but it also burns out the fire and makes it become hollow before the metal has the welding heat. There is a right and a wrong way of taking a welding heat from the fire to the anvil. The pieces must be lifted clear up out of the fire, and must not be dragged thru the dirt and cinders on the inner edge of the fire. Iron will not unite when dirty. It is very easy to get a clean heat if one will pay attention to having the fire clean. Do not attempt to get the welding heat in a dirty fire; this is one thing that must be impressed upon the mind of one working at the forge. The skillful worker in iron always pays particular attention to the fire, for he knows by experience that it must be clean, in order to do good work.

Welding is also done with an electric welding machine. The pieces to be welded are clamped and held in bronze clamps. The clamps are adjusted so that the ends of the pieces to be welded touch. They can be moved so as to bring the pieces into close contact or separate them. When the pieces are in close contact, the current is turned on. The pieces are then separated a little so that the current jumps across the space between them, forming an electric arc. This heats the ends to a welding heat, and by forcing them together they are welded.

Another form of welding is by the oxy-acetylene gas method. It is being used extensively at present, and has been found very valuable and economical in making the lighter welds. It is possible to weld steel, iron, cast-iron, copper, brass and aluminum by this process. The apparatus consists of a specially designed blow pipe, an acetylene tank and an oxygen tank under pressure.

The method of welding is to heat the pieces to be welded with the blow pipe until they reach the fusion point. For instance, in welding cast-iron, the pieces are clamped together, a V shape is cut nearly thru the joint, the metal is heated to the fusion point, and a feeder, which is a small cast-iron rod, is melted into it. In welding steel, the feeder is a steel rod; for copper or brass welding, a rod of copper or brass is used. Nowadays this method is extensively used in automobile work, in repairing cracked cylinders.

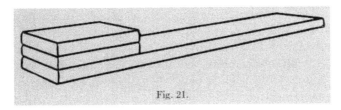

Fig. 21.

A very simple weld to make by heating in the forge, is what is known as the fagot weld. In doing this, two or three pieces are welded by simply laying one piece on top of the other, or a bundle of pieces of iron of various sizes and shapes are bound together, heated and welded. For example, if a bar of flat iron is heated and cut half thru in several places, doubled over and over, one piece on top of the other and then welded in order to make a large piece of stock this would be called a fagot weld.

In Figure 21, the pieces are represented ready to make a fagot weld.

The welding of two pieces of stock by scarfing and lapping is known as a separate-heat-weld, so called because the pieces are detached while the heat is taken. In making any kind of a weld there is more or less stock wasted in the raising of the welding heat, therefore the parts to be lapped and welded are always upset or thickened and then scarfed. The word "scarfed" means the shaping of the ends of the bars so that when heated and lapped one on top of the other, they will fit and make a splice, leaving the stock when hammered about its original size.

The method of upsetting is to heat the ends of the bar, then set the hot end on the anvil with the bar vertical and hammer on the other end. This thickens the heated end. If it is a long heavy bar, the worker churns the bar up and down striking the hot end on the anvil. A bar may also be heated on the end, then fastened in a vise and the hot part hammered to thicken it. In upsetting, the bar must be kept straight as hammering will bend it where heated; if not kept straight, it will not thicken.

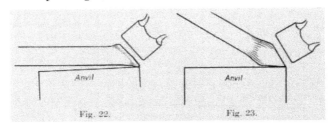

Fig. 22. Fig. 23.

When a piece is upset about one inch in diameter for a three-quarter inch, round bar, it is scarfed by setting the hot end on and near the outer edge of the anvil. It is then driven back on a bevel by hammering. See Figure 22. It is also turned on the side and beveled on both sides to nearly a point. See Figure 23. The scarf must not be hammered when the piece is held in the center of the anvil, (Figure 24), for the reason that the edge of the hammer comes in contact with the anvil, pecking dents in it or breaking out pieces from the hammer.

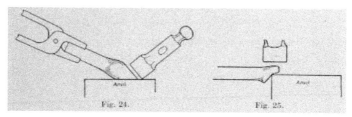

Fig. 24. Fig. 25.

Another method of scarfing is to hammer the end partly back as previously explained, then set the piece on the inner edge of the anvil and hammer it as shown in Figure 25. After each blow, it is drawn away from the edge of the anvil just a little; this tapers it with a series of little steps, not for the purpose of making notches in the scarfs to fit together and hold while hammering, but simply because the edge of the anvil leaves it in this condition when tapered. It is also drawn pointed by hammering on the outer edge of the anvil.

Theory teaches that the scarf should be made with the beveled part convexed. However, in practice, it is made to look like the drawing in Figure 26. Note the raised parts at "D". This is forced up when the scarf is first driven back with the hammer as shown at "B".

The reason that the high part should be on the scarf, is, that when lapped it gives an additional amount of stock at this part of the laps to be hammered. If the scarfs are made flat, when hammered, they are not liable to finish up without having the pieces thin, or the point of the lap exposed. If the scarfs are made concave, it is claimed by some workers of iron that dirt will deposit there and result in a poor weld. This is true to some extent. However, dirt will deposit on any scarf unless the fire is clear. With a concaved scarf when lapped, there is not stock enough to be hammered without leaving the pieces thin, or the lapping too long when welded. Scarfs should not be made concave.

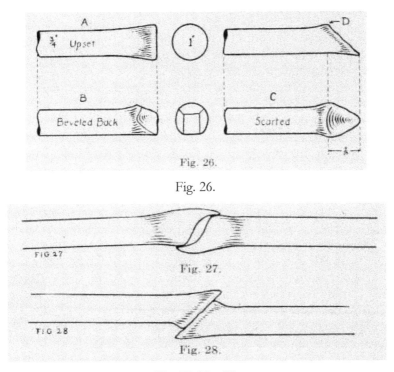

Fig. 26.

Fig. 27. Fig. 28.

Notice in Figure 27, the incorrect way of scarfing and in Figure 28, the correct way.

The scarfs must not be made too long; this is a common fault with all beginners and one to avoid. The scarfs should be made a little longer than the thickness of the iron, perhaps 1½ times the thickness.

In raising the welding heat, the pieces must be placed in the fire with the scarfs, or beveled part, down. The fire must be a clean one. A well burned fire is best. A new fire is not a good one to raise the welding heat in, as there is too much smoke and green coal that comes in contact with the metal. The hammer should be placed on the anvil about over the square hole, so it will be handy to reach when making the weld. The anvil should also be clean. A heavy hammer should be used in welding. The proper way to hold the hand hammer is with the fingers around the handle and the thumb protruding along the side and near the top. The thumb should never grip around the handle, but lie along the side to guide and direct the blows. When using the sledge hammer, stand in front of the anvil and not at its side, and let the first blow be a light one.

In heating a slow blast is maintained. When the pieces begin to get about yellow, more blast is used. The pieces can be watched without removing them from the fire. They should be turned over occasionally, moving them nearer to the surface of fire to see how the heat is progressing, and then under the coke again. Care must be taken to get both pieces heated alike. If one piece should get hotter than the other, it can be moved over in the fire a little, and the cool one put in its place. Perhaps the fire is hotter in one spot than another. If one piece is heating much faster than the other, lift it clear up and out of the fire for a few seconds to cool and give the other piece a chance to become hotter. If the points of the scarf are heating too fast for the body, the pieces must be pushed thru the fire a little farther.

It is a good plan sometimes, when the pieces are about a yellow heat to shut off the wind for a moment, to let the pieces and fire even up and give the heat a chance to soak thru them. As the pieces become nearly white, the blast is increased. Welding heat is about 1900°-2000° Fahrenheit, and can only be determined by experience. When the temperature of the pieces reaches the welding heat, they are lifted up and out of the fire and taken by the smith to the anvil, without the aid of a helper. The smith raps them against one another or against the anvil to dislodge any dirt that may be on the scarfs. The piece in the left hand is set against the inner edge of the anvil. The piece in the right hand is now moved across the anvil until it comes under the top one. See Figure 29. The piece in the left hand is then placed on the under one, by simply raising the hand, teetering the piece on the edge of the anvil, and holding it firmly by pressing down. This is important. The smith lets go of the piece in his right hand, and taking the hammer strikes lightly until the two are stuck, after which he welds them together with solid blows, first on one side, then on the other and finally on the corners.

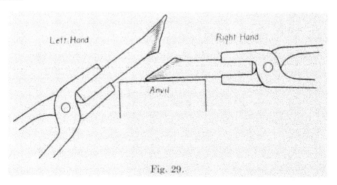

Fig. 29.

It requires some practice to be able to take two pieces from the fire and place them in position on the anvil to be welded. This should be practiced by the pupil under the eye of the teacher, perhaps a dozen or more times, with the cold pieces before he undertakes to get the welding heat. If one cannot take the pieces out and place them in position, he cannot make a weld of this kind.

Two boys should not be allowed to work together on this weld. One can do it much better than two. It is a one-man job. There is nothing difficult about it, after the method is learned by deliberate and persistent practice with the cold iron. There is no need of hurrying when taking the pieces out of the fire to the anvil.

If the scarfs are too long, they will overlap one another too far and cannot be welded down quickly enough. If too short, they hammer down too quickly to make a good job, and the weld will be thin.

If the scarfs are the right length and about the same size, which is important, the weld will finish down in good shape and make a smooth job, providing the ends are clean. When the pieces being heated, look as tho they are covered with grease, you may be sure the fire is dirty, or is too new.

Lap Welding Without Scarfing.

A lap weld is sometimes made without scarfing the ends. For instance, pieces of 1" × ¼" iron are to be welded by the lap method. They are brought to a welding heat without upsetting; taken to the anvil as previously explained for the scarf weld, lapped about $\frac{5}{16}$-inch, as shown in Figure 30, and welded. This form of welding is used in a hurry-up job where there is no great amount of strain on the work. It is impossible to make a strong weld this way. Very thin stock, either iron or steel, can be welded to advantage in this manner by hammering on the flat sides. The edges, instead of being hammered, are cut off with a chisel, then ground or filed smooth. In welding very thin stock, a little flux is used. Always weld by separate heats, and do not rivet or split the stock to hold both ends in place. This is not necessary. Try to make the weld with one heat. All good welds are made in one heat.

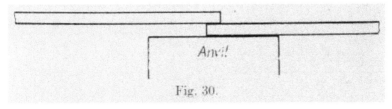

Fig. 30.

Jump Welding.

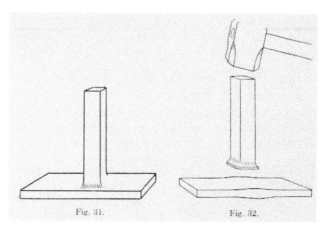

Fig. 31. Fig. 32.

For example, a piece like the one shown in Figure 31, is to be made by welding. The pieces should be prepared as shown in Figure 32. The square piece is 1" by 1" by 6", the flat one 1½" by ½" by 8". The square piece is heated directly on one end. If the heat cannot be taken short enough, it may be cooled in water so as to upset it with a lip or projection, as shown. This lip can be worked out afterwards with a fuller, or it may be driven into a heading tool which has the top corners of the hole rounded. This will leave the corners of the lip round as shown. The bar at the end should also be made slightly convex, so that the center part comes in contact with the flat piece first. The flat piece is also upset in the center.

In welding, separate heats are taken. With the square bar, handled with the right hand, the pieces are brought to the anvil by the smith. The square bar is set on top of the flat one, and a helper strikes the top piece with the sledge, driving it down into the bottom one. The edge of the lip is then welded fast with a hand-hammer; or a fuller or set hammer is used, the helper striking with a sledge.

Butt Weld.

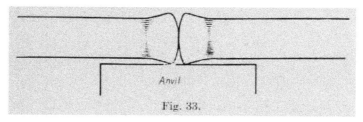

Fig. 33.

Iron may be welded by butting the ends together. In doing this, the bars must be long enough so that they can be handled without tongs. For instance, two bars of one-inch round stock, one five feet long and the other shorter are to be welded. This size is about as light as can be welded with this method. The ends are heated and upset a little making them a little high in the center so that when they are placed together, the contact is in the center. A short heat is taken on the end of each bar. The smith takes out the long bar and the helper the short one, butting the ends together on the anvil, as shown in Figure 33. The helper hammers on the end of the short piece with a heavy hammer while the smith holds the long one firmly, and hammers on the joint, at the same time turning the bar so as to hammer the joint all around. In welding heavier stock, a sledge should be used requiring more helpers. This method makes a good weld, providing the heats are clean.

Split Welding.

Figure 34 shows a drawing of round stock prepared for a split weld. In making this weld, one piece is heated on the end, caught in a vise and split with a thin chisel. See Figure 35.

These prongs are then spread and scarfed on the inside with the ball of the hammer letting them become fan shape and as wide as possible. See Figure 36. The other piece is upset and both pieces are caught in the vise. The scarf is then hammered tight and the ends are cut so as not to have them too long. See Figure 37. The cutting of the scarf, and partly into the bar, helps to bind the pieces firmly while the heat is being taken. See drawing of piece ready to be welded, Figure 38.

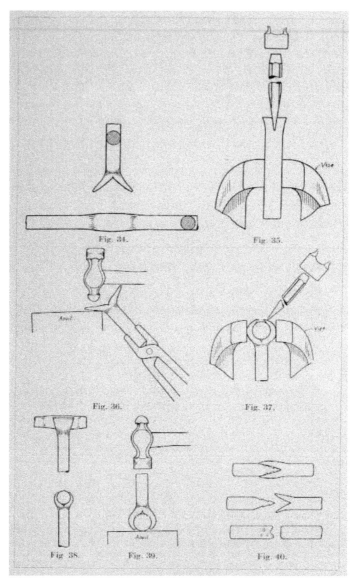

Fig. 34. Fig. 35.

Fig. 36. Fig. 37.

Fig. 38. Fig. 39. Fig. 40.

A heat is now taken, using a little sand or welding flux, if the stock is very small. In welding, the first blow is struck on the end of the split piece to drive it down tight and weld it in the center. See Figure 39. The sides are next hammered to weld the laps. It is then finished. On heavy work, the heats are taken separately and placed on the anvil by the smith, in the same manner as described for a jump weld. Another form of split welding is shown in Figure 40. This method is used in welding heavy iron and steel, such as picks and drills. Notice the little beards cut with a chisel to help hold the pieces in position when heating. Heavy tool steel is also welded with this form of splitting. The first blow struck with the hammer on this weld, is on the end, forcing the pieces together; then on the flat part.

Corner Weld.

In Figure 41 is shown an angle made by welding on the corner; this is called a corner weld. It is generally made by using square or flat stock. Figure 42 shows the scarfs prepared for a corner weld, using 1" by ½" stock. The piece at "A" is scarfed with the ball of the hammer. The one at B, with the face of the hammer. Separate heats are taken and the pieces lapped and welded.

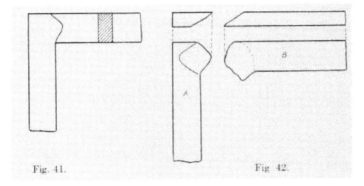

Fig. 41. Fig. 42.

T-Weld.

The scarfs for T-welds are made in just the same manner as for the corner weld, excepting that one scarf is in the center of the bar. See Figure 43.

In taking the pieces from the fire to the anvil, the one scarfed in the center is handled with the tongs in the left hand. The one scarfed on the end is handled with the right hand, letting it under the other, and then hammered. Notice how wide the scarf is made on the end piece at "A". This is done to cover the other scarf. All flat "T" scarfs are made in this manner.

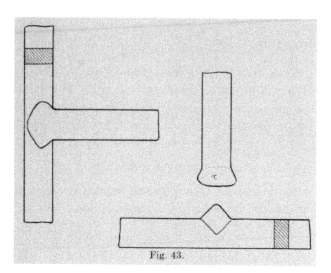

Fig. 43.

CHAPTER III.

Corner Weld—Brazing—Fagot Weld—Turning a Loose Eye—Hammock Hook—Finishing Wrought Iron—S Link—Welded Eye Pin.

A corner weld made by using heavy stock, for example, one and one-fourth inch square, is to have a square corner by welding. See Figure 44. With the dimensions six inches from one end, the bar is heated and cut about half thru from one side with a hot chisel. The bar is then heated and bent to about a right angle, as shown in Figure 45. A piece of ¾-in. square stock is cut on four sides as shown in Figure 46. This piece is welded into the corner as shown in Figure 47. The heat is separate, and the smith takes both pieces to the anvil when hot. He places them in position as shown in the drawing, the helper doing the welding. The long part of the bar is then broken off, another heat is taken and the corner is finished up by the smith.

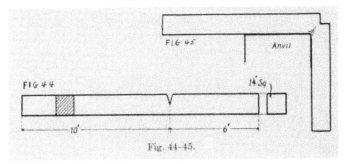

Fig. 44-45.

Brazing.

Iron and steel can be fastened together by brazing. In doing this, the ends are tapered or dove-tailed together and bound with wire or a rivet to hold them in position. They are then placed in the fire and brought to a red heat. Some borax and spelter are put on and the heat is raised until the brass flows. The work is then taken out of the fire and let cool; then it is finished with a file, or by grinding. Spelter is an alloy of copper and zinc, and may be purchased from dealers. Brass wire may also be used in brazing, and sometimes copper.

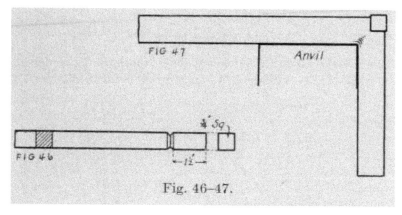

Fig. 46-47.

In teaching boys forging, the writer feels that it is a waste of time to give a beginner little pieces to make, such as staples, hooks, etc. A boy cannot learn to handle his hammer, or to heat a piece of stock by making small things. What the beginner in forging needs is some work that he can swing a hammer on without danger of spoiling it. Very few boys on entering a shop can handle a hammer, and they certainly do not learn about heating metal in a forge, by working at staples, etc. The first exercise should be a fagot weld.

Exercise No. 1.—Fagot Weld.

In doing this, two pieces of iron ½ in. square and 6 in. long are used. The instructor demonstrates the welding of these two pieces before the class. In making the weld, one piece is laid on top of the other and both are caught at one end with a pair of tongs. The tongs should fit the pieces nicely; a ring is placed over the ends of handles to bind the jaws firmly on to the pieces. A heat is then taken on about one-half of the length of the stock; the pieces are welded and at the same time drawn to ½ in. square. The pieces are now turned around in the tongs and the balance is heated and welded. While drawing stock always have the bar at right angles with the long side of the anvil. If the bar is not so held, it will twist on the slightly rounded face of the anvil.

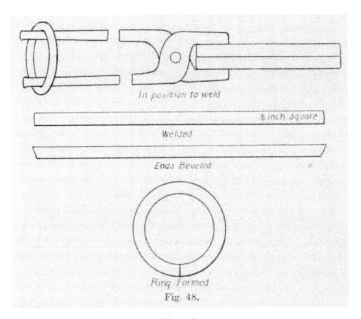

In position to weld

½ inch square

Welded

Ends Beveled

Ring Formed

Fig. 48.

Fig. 48.

There will be more or less iron burned by the boys in making this fagot weld; but this is necessary, for a boy can never learn how to work iron until he can heat it properly. He must over-heat and burn iron in order to understand the heat limitations of the metal.

After the weld is made and the bar is drawn to the original size, the ends must be squared by upsetting them. The bar when finished should be ½ in. square thruout its length, and straight with the ends squared.

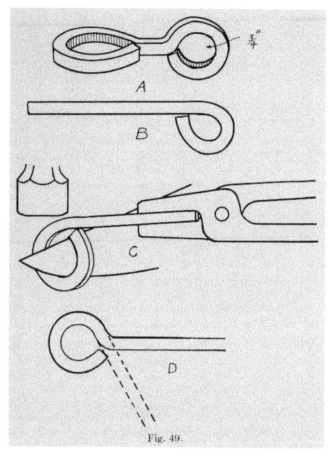

Fig. 49.

It is then formed into a loose ring by hammering it over the horn of the anvil and not on a ring mandrel. In forming the ring, the ends are upset on an angle, so that when bent into ring form, they will fit together nicely. See Figure 48.

Exercise No. 2.

This exercise will be made in the same manner as number one, excepting that the bar is finished to $7/16$ in. square, and a ring is turned on each end. See Figure 49.

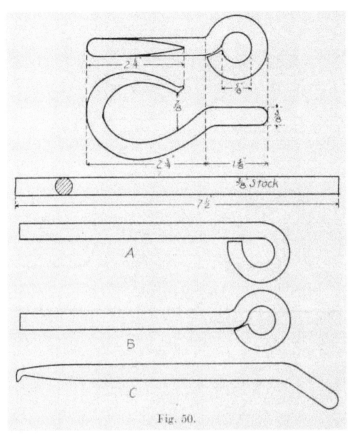

Fig. 50.

The eye is formed by heating and hammering it over the horn of the anvil, giving it the shape as shown at B. It is then reheated, set on the horn of the anvil and hammered close to the eye as shown at C, which bends it central with the shank as shown at D.

In turning loose eyes of any size stock or dimensions, on the end of a bar, the ring is first turned into a circle of the desired size. It is then sprung central with the shank. With this method, no figuring of stock is required.

Exercise No. 3.

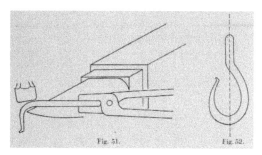

Fig. 51. Fig. 52.

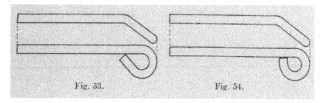

Fig. 53. Fig. 54.

In making a hammock hook, the stock should be soft steel, which may be purchased for about the same price as iron. It will stand the bending strains better than iron. The size of the stock is 7½ in. by ⅜ in. round. The end is heated and a loose eye formed. The other end is drawn to a taper with ¼ in. of the end turned up as shown. See drawing of hook, Figure 50, and the different steps in forming the eye at A, B and C. The hook is formed over the horn of the anvil as shown in Figure 51. Figure 52 shows the finished hook with a dotted line drawn thru the center, indicating where the pull should come. In Figure 53 is shown a common fault when turning a loose ring at the end of a bar, in not bending the extreme end first. Notice Figure 54, where the end is bent as it should be.

The expert worker in iron is very careful not to hammer mark and destroy the section of a bar. One should remember that bending a ring or iron hook is simply holding the bar on the horn of the anvil and striking the part that protrudes past it. Never strike the bar when it is directly over the horn. This does not bend it, but makes a dent in the stock.

Finishing.

To finish wrought iron, all of the scale and dirt should be scraped off with an old file while the piece is hot. When the iron is cooled, linseed or machine oil is rubbed on. If the work is held over the smoke of the fire and then oiled, it will take on a darker color. Never paint iron work. This destroys the texture of the metal. Do not file work bright. It should be dark—filing is not forging.

Exercise No. 4.— S-Link.

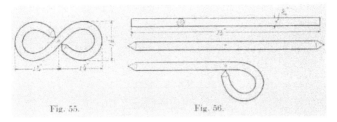

Fig. 55. Fig. 56.

Figure 55 shows a drawing of an S-Link, which is used to splice broken chains. In Figure 56 is shown he length and size of the stock. The ends are drawn to a short point and the center of the bar is marked with a center punch. One-half of the link is then formed, bringing the point at the center punch mark and using one-half of the bar. This is a simple link to make. The only thing to be careful about is to not destroy the section of the bar with hammer marks. This may be avoided if one does not strike the hook directly over the horn of the anvil, but to one side of the horn. See in Figure 57, the correct blow.

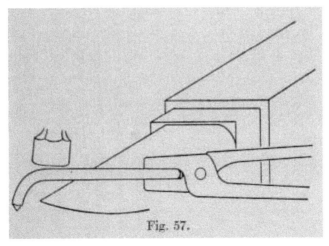

Fig. 57.

Exercise No. 5.

Figure 58 shows a drawing for a welded Eye Pin. The eye may be made any size for practice. In making the ring, the bar is heated in the center and hammered over the outer edge of the anvil, as shown in Figure 59. The piece is now turned end for end, and jogged down again with the ball of the hammer. See Figure 60. The piece should now look like the drawing in Figure 61. The center of the piece is heated and hammered over the horn of the anvil to make the ring round and to bring the shanks together. See Figure 62.

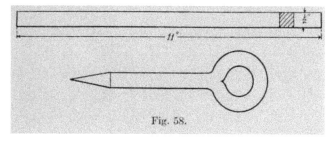

Fig. 58.

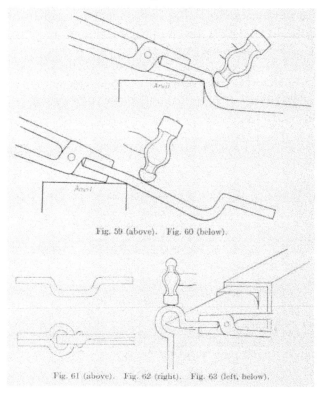

Fig. 59 (above). Fig. 60 (below).

Fig. 61 (above). Fig. 62 (right). Fig. 63 (left, below).

In welding, the piece is caught by the ring with a flat pair of tongs. See Figure 63. It is now placed in the fire so as to get the heat close to the ring. The tongs are then removed, until the piece reaches a white heat; the piece is again caught with the tongs, and the heat is raised. It is taken out and set on the edge of the anvil and hammered as shown in Figure 64. The first blow struck is close to the ring in order to weld that part first. If it cannot be all welded in one heat, it should be reheated at once. Do not hammer unless the heat is a welding heat, as the stock will become too thin before it is welded. Do not heat the tongs red as this destroys them and the piece cannot be held with hot tongs. When the ring is welded, the end is drawn to a square point. See Figure 65.

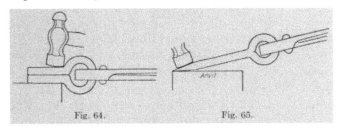

Fig. 64. Fig. 65.

CHAPTER IV.

Staples—Open Links—Welded Chain Links—Punching—A Grab Hook.

Exercise No. 6.

Staples are used for hasps, gate hooks, and for various other purposes. They are made from all sizes of stock, depending on the use to which they are put. On account of its pliability, soft steel is the best stock to use in making staples.

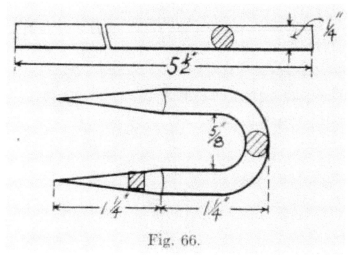

Fig. 66.

Fig. 66.

The length to cut stock is shown in the drawing of the staple in Figure 66. The stock is caught at one end with a pair of light tongs. The piece is then heated and drawn out to a point; it is reversed in the tongs and the other end is drawn out. The center of the piece is then reheated and bent into shape over the horn of the anvil.

In drawing any piece of stock to a tapered point, the taper should not be hammered on one side continuously and, when turned over, hammered back again. To have a taper on all four sides alike, the bar must be raised the proper distance and not laid flat on the anvil. Figure 67 illustrates the wrong way and Figure 68, the correct way.

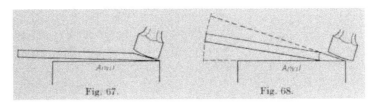

Fig. 67. Fig. 68.

Exercise No. 7.

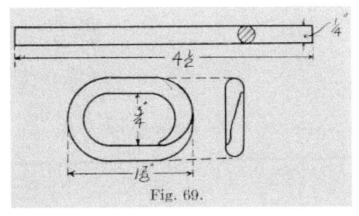

Fig. 69.

Fig. 70. Fig. 71.

In Figure 69 is shown a drawing of an open link. Open links are used in the splicing of broken chains. In splicing a chain, the link is opened by driving a chisel between the laps, or it is opened when made. These laps are hooked into links of broken chain and then driven together. In making the link, one end is drawn to a flat point and a hook is hammered on it. See Figure 70. The other end is heated and drawn out as in Figure 71. The center of the piece is now heated and bent over the horn of the anvil to the desired shape. See Figure 72. Notice in the drawing that the hooks at the open end of the link are not very long. They should not be made longer than shown.

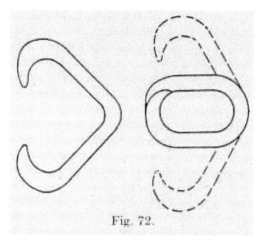

Fig. 72.

Exercise No. 8.—Welding a Chain Link.

The form and length of the stock for this exercise is shown in Figure 73. The link may be made from iron or soft steel. After the stock is cut, it is heated in the center and bent over the horn of the anvil into a "U" shape. See Figure 74. The ends are now heated and scarfed by setting them on the anvil as shown in Figure 75. The iron is then struck on top with the hand hammer. After each blow, it is moved away from the anvil just a little, giving the end a bevel, so that, when finished, the scarf consists of a series of slanting notches.

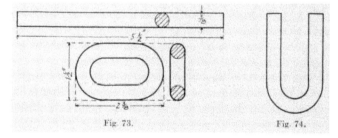

Fig. 73. Fig. 74.

In scarfing, both ends of the links are set on the anvil. The end of the one on the right hand side must not be moved when scarfing the other. After each blow of the hammer, the piece is moved just a little. If it is moved too far and the other end of the link is fixed it will describe an arc. See Figure 76. This is the method used in scarfing links. Sometimes they are welded without scarfing, but it is not good practice.

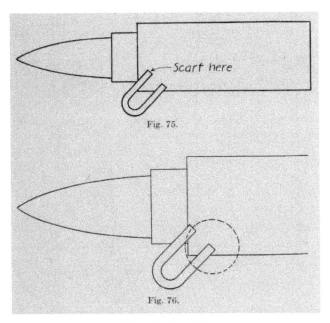

Fig. 75. Fig. 76.

Figure 77 shows the link scarfed, lapped and ready to be welded. In welding, the heat is taken directly on the end of the lap and not on the sides, so as not to burn the stock above the laps. When the link has the welding heat, it is taken to the anvil and hammered on the flat sides, then set on the horn of the anvil, and hammered on the corners. See Figure 78. The shape of the link at the weld should be just a little pointed for a strong link.

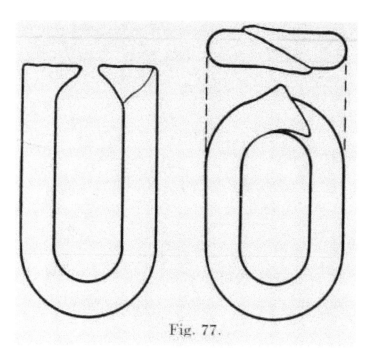

Fig. 77.

In making chains, do not weld two single links and then one between them. Weld a link on the end of the chain and keep repeating until finished.

Exercise No. 9.

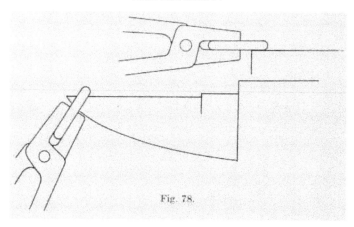

Fig. 78.

Punching holes thru hot iron is not a difficult exercise. For instance: A ³⁄₈-in. hole is to be punched thru a flat piece of iron or steel. The piece is heated, taken to the anvil and a punch set on the spot to be punched. The punch is struck three or four blows with the hand hammer driving it into the metal as shown in Figure 79. The piece is then turned over and the punch is set over the dark spot which is caused by the former blows, and is driven thru. See Figure 80. Square and other shaped holes are punched in the same manner. Thin stock is punched cold. In doing this, the piece to be punched is set on the punch block and the punch driven thru the metal into the hole of the block. A punch-block is a round or square block of steel with one or more tapered holes thru it. See Figure 81.

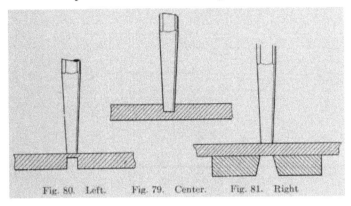

Fig. 80. Left. Fig. 79. Center. Fig. 81. Right.

Figure 82 shows some holes that could be punched while the metal is hot. A hole like the one shown at A, is made with a punch of that shape; the next hole is made with the same punch. Afterwards the hole is upset or shortened by heating and cooling each side of the hole. The bar is then hammered on the end. This shortens and spreads the metal. The hole is made true by driving a round punch thru it. The stock used for this exercise should be soft steel.

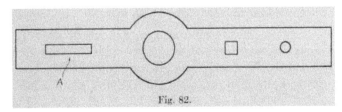

Fig. 82.

Exercise No. 10.—A Grab Hook for a Log Chain.

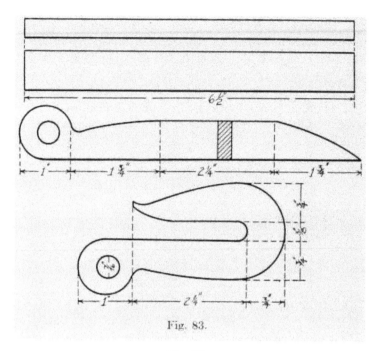

Fig. 83.

Fig. 83.

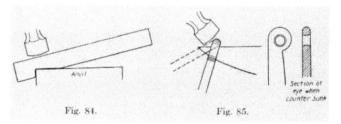

Fig. 84.   Fig. 85.

Fig. 84. Fig. 85.

Figure 83 shows a drawing of the hook with size of stock to be used. The stock should be mild steel, 6½ by ¾ by ⅜ inches. To form the eye one end is heated and shouldered back one inch from the end, by hammering it on the anvil as shown in Figure 84. The eye is then rounded with the hammer and the hole punched with a hand punch. The hole is countersunk by hammering it on the horn as shown in Figure 85. The point is next drawn out and then the hook is heated in the center. It is cooled each side of the center and hammered over the horn to bend, then on the anvil as shown at Figure 86. A piece of ⅜-in. flat iron is set on the inside of the hook and the hook hammered to fit the iron. This leaves the opening of the hook uniform and just the size required. See Figure 87.

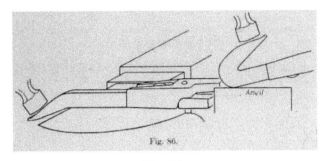

Fig. 86.

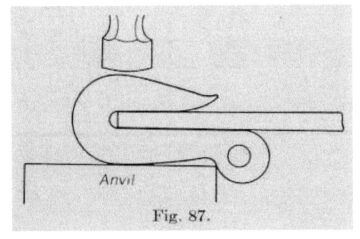

Fig. 87.

CHAPTER V.

Bolts—Capping Tool—Gate Hook—Hay Hook—Welded Ring—Expansion of Heated Iron.

Exercise No. 11.

Bolts may be made in one piece by upsetting the end of a bar, then squaring the head by driving the piece into a heading tool. A bolt may also be made by welding a collar around the end of a bar after which the head is squared.

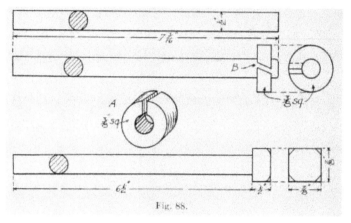

Fig. 88.

Figure 88 shows a welded bolt head. After the stock is cut to proper length, the collar for the head is made. It is heated and hammered over the horn of the anvil to make it round. The end of the collar is now cut off on the hardie, cutting clear thru from one side and giving it a bevel. The other end is cut from the opposite side giving it a bevel also. See drawing at A. The collar is driven on the end of the bar while the collar is cold and the bar is hot. When the collar is hammered on the end of the bar, there should be about ⅛-in. crack. See drawing at B. The reason is that, in welding, the collar is lengthened. Hammering stretches the metal, and it must have end room. When the collar is ready the bar is heated on the end and upset just a little. A heat is then taken, and the collar is welded by striking it on four sides, letting the opening form one of the corners. The bolt is then inserted into a ½-in. hole in a heading tool to smooth the end of the head with a hammer. A cupping tool is next set on to the head and given a few good blows with the hammer. This bevels the top corners of the square head. A cupping tool is a piece of tool steel with a half round depression in one end. See Figure 89.

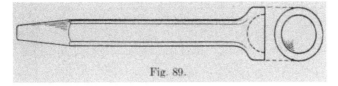

Fig. 89.

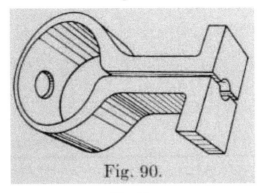

Fig. 90.

The heads of bolts can be beveled with the hammer, instead of with a cupping tool. Figure 90 shows a tool to be used in the vise to make heads on light rods. The rod is heated and inserted into the hole; then the vise is tightened after which the ends are hammered down.

Exercise No. 12.—Forging a Gate Hook.

Figure 91 shows the length and size of stock which should be of soft steel. One and one-half inches from each end of the bar is marked with a center punch. One end is drawn round to a point. The other is hammered round for the eye. See Figure 92. In the drawing Figure 93, the eye and the hook are shown turned. The center part of the hook is square and is to be twisted. This is done by heating the square part to a uniform heat and cooling each end. The hook is then twisted with two pairs of tongs, or it may be caught in a vise and twisted with one pair of tongs. See drawing of the finished hook, Figure 94.

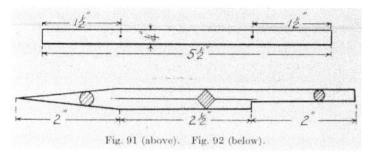

Fig. 91 (above). Fig. 92 (below).

Fig. 91 (above). Fig. 92 (below).

Fig. 93. Fig. 94.

Fig. 93. Fig. 94.

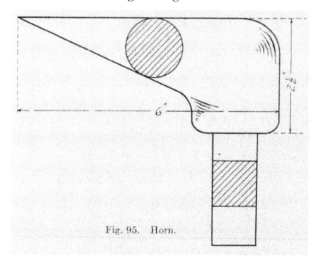

Fig. 95. Horn.

Fig. 95. Horn.

Figure 95 shows a tool called a horn; it fits into the square hole of the anvil. It is used to turn very small eyes at the end of a bar. A piece of 1½-in. round soft steel is used in making it, by drawing the end square to fit the hole in the anvil. It is afterwards bent over and the taper drawn as shown.

Exercise No. 13—Making a Hay Hook.

Figure 96 shows the stock which should be soft steel, to be used in making a Hay Hook. The eye is first turned, using 11 inches of the bar. The end is then heated and drawn to a point after which it is bent as shown in the drawing.

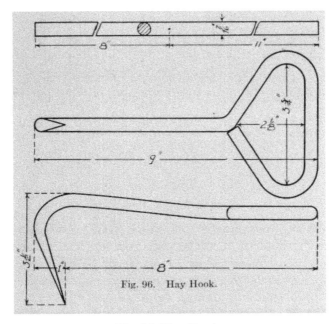

Fig. 96. Hay Hook.

Fig. 96. Hay Hook.

Exercise No. 14—Welding Ring.

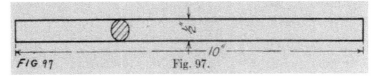

Fig. 97.

Fig. 97.

Figure 97 shows a drawing for a ring to be made from ½-in. round stock cut 10 inches long. The whole is heated red at one time and then formed into shape by hammering it over the horn as shown in Figure 98. The ends are now heated and scarfed in the same manner as described for the welded link. When they are lapped and ready for welding, they should look like Figure 99. Notice that the ring is made egg shape so that a heat may be taken directly on the ends of the scarfs and not at the sides. The ring when welded is formed round.

Another method of welding rings is to upset the ends and then form the rings. It is scarfed as explained above. This is seldom done in practical work because it is too slow, and the other method is about as strong.

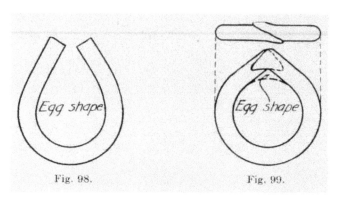

Fig. 98. Fig. 99.

In welding the ring, it is handled in the same manner as in welding links. To find the amount of stock for rings, the inside diameter plus the thickness of stock is multiplied by 3.1416 or 3□. To this is added enough stock for the lap of the weld. For example a ring is required of one-inch stock. The inside measure is 10 inches. Solution: $(10 + 1) \times 3□ = 11 \times 3□ = 34^4/_7 + \frac{1}{2}$ inch for welding.

In heating a piece of iron to be formed into a ring, it should never be heated to the welding heat. A welding heat on any piece of work that is not to be hammered destroys the texture of the metal. Any piece of work to be formed, should be heated evenly and not too hot.

Iron when heated expands. For example, if a piece of stock 12 by 1 by $^5/_{19}$ in. is heated red its entire length and then measured, it will be about $12\frac{1}{4}$ in. long. When the piece is cooled it will go back to its original length of twelve inches.

In making bands or tires for wagons, they are made a little short, then heated and put on, letting them shrink to their original size, which makes them tight.

Wrought Iron Lantern.

CHAPTER VI.

Marking Tongs—Pig Iron—Puddling—The Bessemer Process—The Open Hearth Process—Crucible Steel—The Cementation Process—Tempering.

Exercise No. 16.

In forging tongs, stock ⅞-in. square of Norway or Swedish iron may be used, as it is much easier for a beginner in welding the handle on to the jaws. Soft steel may be used later on if desired. Figure 100 shows the drawing of a finished pair of flat tongs. Figure 101 shows the size of stock used and the dimensions of the rough forgings. It is not intended that the dimensions given are to be accurately followed, but they are given as an idea of what may be forged from this size of stock. In forging the jaws, no helper is required to handle a sledge hammer after the piece is cut from the bar for the reason that it is time lost for the one who handles it, besides one man can do it.

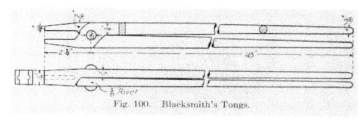

Fig. 100. Blacksmith's Tongs.

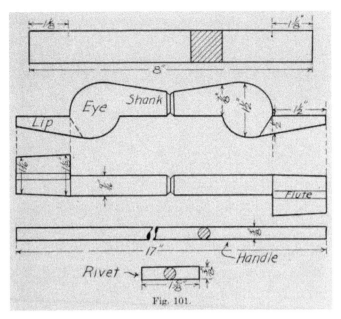

Fig. 101.

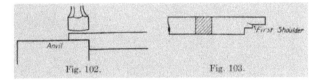

Fig. 102. Fig. 103.

In forging the jaws a heavy hand hammer is used, and the bar is heated to the welding heat, or near it. One and one-eighth inch of the bar is set on the inner edge of the anvil and the lip is hammered as shown in Figure 102. The lip must not be turned and hammered on its edge. Let it get as wide as it will, and do not hammer it too thin. After the shoulder has been started for the length of the lip, it must not be moved. A common fault is to start the shoulder and then to find that the lip is not long enough and proceed to make another shoulder. The result of the second shoulder is that when nearly finished a crack will be discovered. The reason that second shoulder starts a crack is that the metal stretched over the first shoulder. This is called a cold shut. See Figure 103. Another common fault is to lower the bar when making the lip. This pulls the lip on an angle with the bar and when it is straightened, another crack is formed in the corner. See Figure 104. The bar must be on the same plane with the anvil face at all times. When the lip is made, the bar is turned to the left, setting it on the outer edge of the anvil and hammering to form the shoulder for the eye. See

Figure 105. It is then turned again to the left hand and hammered down for the last shoulder.

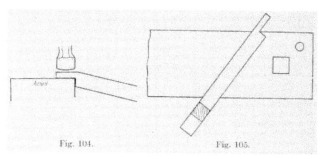

Fig. 104. Fig. 105.

At this time the stock required for the eye is beyond the outer edge of the anvil. See Figure 106.

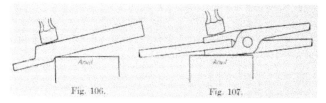

Fig. 106. Fig. 107.

The rough forging should always be made a little larger than the finished tongs; finishing it to size when the handle is welded on. When both jaws are forged, they are cut in the center and the handles are welded on. When the handles are well upset and scarfed, the shanks of the jaws are drawn to equal size. Care must be taken in having the scarfed ends equal in size or a poor weld will result. The handles at the weld are drawn square with the corners tapered off. The jaws are now drawn and fitted to size. Notice that the lip tapers on the edge, also on the flat part. A small flute is fullered lengthways on the inside of the lip so that round as well as flat iron may be held. The hole is next punched thru the eye with a hand punch. A piece of ⅜-in. rod of soft steel is cut to the proper length and used for a rivet. It is heated and inserted into the holes in the jaws and hammered on both sides with hard blows. The jaws of the tongs are now heated red and worked back and forth to loosen the rivet in the eye. The jaws are fitted to the size of the stock they are to handle as in Figure 107. The regular stock rivets should not be used in tongs. The ⅜-in. round piece headed from both sides fits the holes thru the eye best.

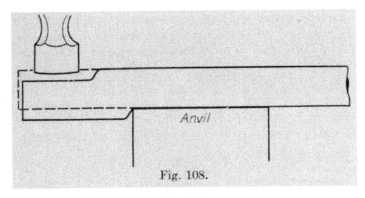

Fig. 108.

In making tongs to hold a larger piece of stock, the square bar should have an offset. The jaws should then be forged as in Figure 108. Notice where the hammer strikes the bar to offset it.

In forging tongs, the handles should be welded to the jaws to give practice in welding.

Pig Iron.

Pig iron is made by smelting the iron ore in a blast furnace. The ore is charged in a furnace mixed with lime stone as a flux, and melted by using coke or coal as fuel. The resulting metal is called pig iron. It contains from three to five per cent of carbon, two to four per cent of silicon and various small amounts of sulphur, phosphorus and manganese.

Puddling.

Wrought iron is made by melting the pig iron in a puddling furnace; about one-half ton is charged at a time. After it is softened, it is stirred with large iron hooks by the puddler and his helper. It is kept kneaded to expose every part to the action of the flame, so as to burn out all of the carbon. All the other impurities separate from the iron and form what is known as the puddle clinker.

Pig iron melts at about 2100° F., steel at 2500° F., and wrought iron at 2800° F., so the temperature of the puddling furnace is kept high enough to melt pig iron but not hot enough to keep wrought iron in a liquid state. Consequently, as soon as the iron becomes pure it forms a spongy mass. This mass of sponge is divided into lumps of about 100 or 150 pounds which are taken to a squeezer and formed into blocks. In the operation of squeezing the greater proportion of impurities left in the iron after the puddling, are removed. While these blocks are still hot they are rolled into flat musk bars. The bars are now cut and heated to white heat in a furnace, taken to the rolls, welded and rolled into merchant bars. In the welding and rolling the cinder coated globules of iron are forced close together as the iron is welded. This gives the iron a fibrous structure increasing its strength.

Bessemer Process.

In making steel by the Bessemer process, the pig iron is put into a large pear shaped vessel called the converter. The bottom is double; the inner casing is perforated with holes called tuyeres, to admit air forced under pressure. From ten to fifteen tons of molten iron at one time are poured into the converter while it is lying on its side. The compressed air is now turned into the double bottom as the converter rises to a vertical position. The air has sufficient pressure to prevent the metal from entering the tuyeres, and it passes up and thru the metal, burning out the carbon. After the blast which lasts about ten minutes, the metal is practically liquid wrought iron. The converter is now laid on its side and the blast is shut off. A certain amount of molten spiegeleisen (white cast iron containing much carbon or ferromanganese) is added so as to give the steel the proper amount of carbon and manganese to make it suitable for its purpose. The steel is then poured into ingots and rolled into rails, girders, etc. Carbon is pure charcoal; manganese is a chemical element very difficult to fuse, but easily oxidized.

Open Hearth Process.

The open hearth process of steel manufacturing is similar to the puddling process. The carbon is removed by the action of an oxidizing flame of burning gas. The furnace has a capacity of forty or fifty tons and is heated with gas or oil. The gas and air needed for its combustion are heated to a temperature of over 1000° F. before entering the combustion chamber, by passing thru so-called regenerative chambers. Owing to the preheating of the gas and air a very high temperature can be maintained in the furnace so as to keep the iron liquid after it has parted with the carbon. The stirring up of the metal is not done with hooks as in puddling furnace but by adding certain proportions of iron scales or other oxides the chemical reaction of which keeps the metal in a state of agitation. With the open hearth process the metal can be tested from time to time. When it contains the proper amount of carbon it is drawn off thru the tapping hole at the bottom of the hearth, leaving the slag at the top. As steel is produced in a liquid form, from which impurities have been removed in the form of slag that rises and floats at the top, the metal is homogeneous and practically without grain. Wrought iron will outlast steel when exposed to the weather.

Crucible steel, or tool steel, also called cast steel, is made by using high grade, Swedish, wrought iron and adding carbon which is low in phosphorus content. The oldest method is called the "Cementation

Process." The iron bars were packed in air-tight retorts with powdered charcoal between them. They were put in a cementation furnace, heated red and kept at this temperature for several days. The bars, in this way, absorbed the carbon from the charcoal. The carbonized bars (called "blister steel") were then cut into small pieces, remelted in a crucible, poured in ingots and rolled into bars.

The newer method is to melt small pieces of Norway or Swedish iron base with charcoal in a graphite or clay crucible. It is then poured into moulds and made into ingots, after which it is forged or rolled into bars.

The crucible process enables the manufacture of steel to almost exact analysis and insures a clean and pure material. It also absorbs the carbon much faster than steel made the old way.

In the school forge shop, the tool steel used should be of an inexpensive kind. High priced steel should not be used as more or less is wasted by the pupils in working. A carbon steel should be used for all forge shop tools. About 75 to 95 point is suitable. High-speed tool steel should be used only to give the pupils instruction in its handling and use, and to familiarize them with the different kinds of steel and their treatment.

To the steel maker, temper means the percentage of carbon in the steel. The word point means one-hundredth of one per cent, thus 10 point carbon means ten one-hundredths of one per cent. One hundred and fifty point carbon contains one and one-half per cent. This is about as high as is generally made. One hundred and fifty point is known as high temper; low temper is about 40 point. Steel containing less than 40 point does not harden to advantage and is classed with machinery steel. There is a range of tempers between high and low point which are used for different kinds of tools.

In the forge shop the term *temper* means the degree of hardness given to a piece of tool steel. As an example, a piece of steel is heated to a dark red color and cooled in water or oil. This is called hardening. If this piece is too hard for the purpose intended, it is then tempered to reduce some of its hardness, and to give the steel elasticity and strength. In doing this, it is subjected to heat, (the more heat the softer the piece becomes). In the forge shop, in tempering steel, the metal is polished bright after hardening. If it is a small piece, it is then held on or near a piece of hot iron. As the piece becomes heated, the steel heated in the air assumes colors; at first a very faint yellow and gradually darker, until all of the color has disappeared leaving the steel without any trace of hardness.

These different colors as they appear on the surface of hardened steel represent different degrees of hardness. The following simple list of colors applies to the different tools and carbon to use:

Light straw—430° F. Lathe tools—130 point carbon.

Dark straw—470° F. Taps and dies—120 point carbon.

Purple gray—530° F. Chisels and blacksmiths' tools, 75 to 95 point carbon.

Of course there are other colors than these. As the heat advances every few degrees the color keeps changing to a darker which indicates the tool is becoming softer.

The hardening heat is about 1300 to 1400 degrees Fahrenheit, or a cherry red. About 400 degrees Fahrenheit relieves the strain in a hardened piece of steel; 600 degrees leaves a trace of hardness and is about right for springs.

In order to know the results of heating and cooling steel one should take a small bar and cut nicks in it with a chisel every half inch. The bar is then heated from a white heat at the end to a very dark red some inches back. It is then cooled in water, the pieces broken and the grain noted. The heat that leaves the steel file hard and a very fine grain is the hardening heat of that steel. The hardening heat is a dark red. The hotter it was when cooled the coarser the grain shows on the end of the broken pieces.

In further demonstrating hardening and tempering of tool steel, the making of a flat cold chisel will be considered. The principles involved are about the same in all hardening and tempering.

CHAPTER VII.

**Making a Flat Cold Chisel—Spring Tempering—Welding Steel—
Case Hardening—Coloring Steel—Annealing—Making a Scratch
Awl—Making a Center Punch—Making a Hand Punch—High
Speed Steel—Annealing High Speed Steel.**

Exercise No. 17.—Flat Cold Chisel.

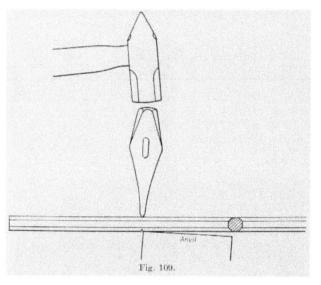

Fig. 109.

A good cold chisel is an indispensable tool in a shop, and one that is very much abused. Therefore, it should be made with the greatest care. In the forging of a good chisel a piece of ⅝-in. octagonal tool steel, from 75 to 95 point carbon, is used. The piece is cut six inches long. In doing this the bar may be nicked with a chisel. The nicked part is then set over the outer edge of the anvil. A chisel with a handle is set on the nicks and given a good blow with a sledge hammer, shearing the piece from the bar. See Figure 109. This method of cutting is quite dangerous, so care must be taken. Perhaps, a less dangerous method, tho not so practical, is to heat the bar red and cut the piece off with a hot chisel and sledge, or on the hardie, if one has no helper. The end is then hammered. See Figure No. 110.

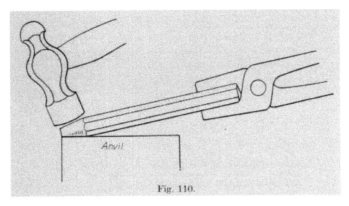

Fig. 110.

When cut off and hammered round on one end, the piece is caught with a fluted-lip pair of tongs that will hold it firmly and a ring is placed on the ends of the reins to bind them. The end is now heated in a well burned fire, letting the heat soak in slowly, and not forcing it with too much blast. If the fire is lively hardly any blast is used on the start. The piece is brought to a heat somewhat beyond what is commonly called cherry heat. It is then taken to the anvil and drawn out square with hard blows of the hammer, to a long taper, and nearly to a point. This taper should be about 1¾ inches long. See Figure No. 111.

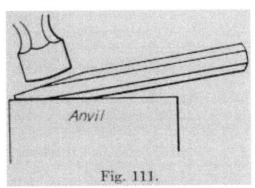

Fig. 111.

Hammering must cease before the red heat has left the steel. It is again heated and hammered on two sides; in drawing the chisel bends edgewise. Do not strike it on the edge; it will fracture the grain of the steel. To straighten the blade, it should be hammered on the *flat* side *near the concave edge*. See Figure No. 112. This stretches the metal and straightens the blade.

Care must be taken in hammering not to make the chisel wider in one place than in another.

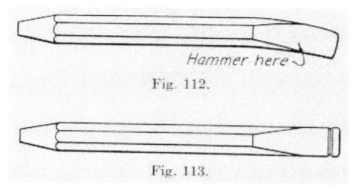

Fig. 112. Fig. 113.

When finishing the chisel, it is hammered lightly until the red is nearly but not quite gone. This hammering packs the grain and makes it fine. The end of the chisel is set on a hardie and cut half thru, so that when it is hardened and tempered it may be broken to note its grain and also require less grinding in sharpening. See Figure No. 113. The chisel is now heated very slowly to a dark red and set in a dry place on the forge to anneal. This annealing relieves the strain in the tool due to hammering.

When the chisel is cold it is reheated to harden and temper. Over-heating does not make the tool harder when cooled in water, but increases its brittleness, so care must be taken when heating. The heating must be very slow, and to a dark red, 2½ inches long. The chisel should be cooled as the heat is going up. A common practice of heating the steel more than a cherry red and holding it out of the forge until the heat goes down, before dipping, is wrong. When properly heated the chisel is held in a vertical position and dipped about 1½ inches into 16 gallons of salt and water, heated from 60° to 70° F. See Figure 114. The tool is kept in motion when dipped. When cooled it is removed, and the hardened part is rubbed bright with an emery stick or sand paper. This is done so that the temper colors may be seen. Tempering increases the tool's elasticity and strength, and reduces the brittleness. The temper color will show just a faint yellow against the edge of the remaining heat that was left in the tool after hardening.

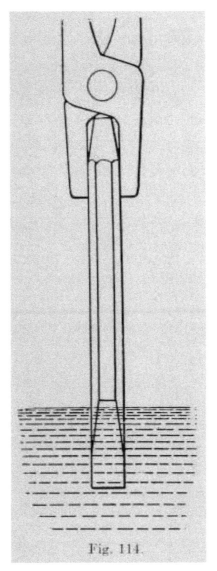

Fig. 114.

In hardening the tool, it is heated 2½ inches of its length and 1½ inches is cooled in water to harden. The remaining heat gradually runs thruout the whole chisel and may be noted by the faint yellow color on the bright part of the tool traveling towards the cutting end. This faint yellow temper color, due to the heat and air, is followed with darker colors; if let run too much all of the hardness would be taken out of the tool. Four hundred and thirty degrees Fahrenheit would be about a light straw color, leaving the steel very hard. About 600° F. would be the darkest color, nearly black.

This is as hot as steel can be made and still leave a trace of hardness. This temper is too soft for a chisel but about right for springs; therefore when the very dark purple temper color covers the whole bright part of the chisel the point is dipped in water. The chisel is then set in a dry place on the forge to cool slowly. The temper color must run to the end of the chisel very slowly. The reason for this is that if the temper color comes slow, the chisel is tempered farther back from the point. The temper colors on the surface of the bright steel are obtained by different degrees of heat, as it travels from the remaining heat left in the tool when the piece was hardened. The less heat allowed to travel toward the end of chisel, the paler the temper color and the harder the chisel; therefore, the faint yellow color indicates that the steel is very hard. The darker the temper color becomes the softer the tool.

The best chisels are those that are file proof. If, after hardening and tempering a chisel, it cannot be cut with a file, it is too hard and the temper must be run out more. If the grain of steel is very fine when broken the chisel had the proper heat when quenched, but if it looks coarse the tool was too hot when cooled and must be annealed, rehardened and tempered. A little judgment will enable one to determine the proper hardness for all tools of this character by noting these temper colors. The above explanation in a general way applies to the working of all carbon steel tools.

Spring Tempering.

There are many kinds of springs that are hardened and tempered. The methods of handling are about the same with all. As an example, a piece of spring steel 5 by 1 by $\frac{1}{16}$ inches is to be tempered. In doing this, the piece is caught at one end with a pair of light tongs. The steel is heated to a dark red and dipped into a can of sperm oil, or equal parts of lard and tallow. When cool it is held over the fire until the surplus oil takes fire and blazes off. It is redipped in the oil, and the oil is burned three times in all. It is then partly cooled in the oil and set on the forge until cool, when it is ready for use. Steel is manufactured especially for springs. It is called spring steel. It is made in a different way from tool steel, by the open hearth process. It differs in quality and cannot be absolutely guaranteed. The steel is never free from all foreign elements which might be detrimental to its quality.

Tempering Thin Pieces of Steel.

In hardening thin pieces of steel such as knives, very thin milling cutters, etc., there is always difficulty in preventing warping after hardening. Two heavy surface plates, planed on one side, are used. On one of these plates equal parts of tallow and lard are spread $\frac{1}{4}$ inch thick. The knife is heated in a steam pipe with one end plugged and having fire under and over it.

When an even red heat is reached, the knife is brought out and set on the oil and at the same time the top plate is set onto the knife until cool. This hardens the blade and keeps it from springing. The knife is brightened and the temper is drawn to a dark straw color by holding it on a hot iron.

Very small pieces of steel are packed into an iron pipe or box surrounded with charcoal. The whole is then heated red and the pieces are dumped out and cooled in water. To draw temper, they are put in an iron ladle filled with lard oil that is heated on the fire.

Welding Steel.

All small pieces of tool and spring steel should be welded with separate heats. A little practice and a clean fire, with some good welding compound, are necessary. In separate heat welding of flat steel, the flat sides of the scarfs are put together instead of the beveled ones. The scarfs are shown in Figure No. 115. The method of riveting and splitting small pieces of flat steel to hold them together while taking the heat is not to be recommended because after they are put together in this manner the lap is double thick, and in raising the heat there is always danger of over-heating each side of the lap. Separate heats and a clean fire is the best method to use to make a good weld, unless the steel is heavy. In this case, it is split and forked as previously explained.

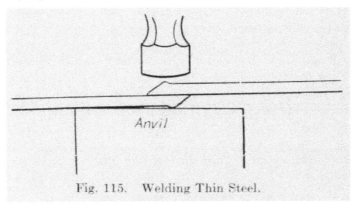

Fig. 115. Welding Thin Steel.

Case Hardening.

The difference between wrought iron and tool steel lies in the absence of carbon in the iron. Tool steel can be hardened because it contains carbon, and when heated and suddenly cooled becomes hard thruout. The surface of wrought iron or mild steel can be carbonized and then made very hard.

This is called *case hardening* because about $\frac{1}{16}$ inch or less of the outside of the bar is made hard while the center is soft. There are several methods. One is to place the articles in a tight cast iron box and surrounded with ground bone before placing in a furnace. The box is then brought to a high heat of about 1700 degrees Fahrenheit. It is held at this heat for several hours and then let cool. When cool, the pieces are reheated and dipped in salt water to harden them or they may be cooled with the first heating. By another method the pieces are placed in an iron ladle with cyanide of potassium and heated. Iron may be heated red and rolled in the cyanide, then reheated and plunged into water. Care must be taken in handling cyanide as even the fumes are poisonous.

Coloring Steel.

Very bright pieces of soft steel can be case hardened and colored at the same time. In doing this, cyanide is heated in an iron box, and the steel articles are put into it. When heated they are removed and dipped into a solution of water and salt peter to cool and harden them. This gives them a mottled effect with many colors. A pint of salt peter to about four gallons of water makes a solution strong enough. This bath becomes poisoned from the cyanide. It should be kept clean and labeled *"Poison."*

Annealing.

A piece of metal of any kind is said to be "annealed" when made very soft. Steel should be annealed before it is filed, drilled, or machined, as it is a very hard metal to work when cold. The method of annealing is first to heat the piece to a red heat. It is then covered with warm, slacked lime so that the air will not come in contact with it until cool. A simple way to anneal, when in a hurry, is to heat the steel red, setting it in a dry place on the forge until black. It is then plunged into water quickly and brought out. This operation is repeated until the piece is cool. Steel is also annealed by heating the piece red and setting it on the forge until cool. The slower steel is cooled, the softer it becomes. Wrought iron and mild steel forgings should always be annealed when used in work where there is danger of breaking them.

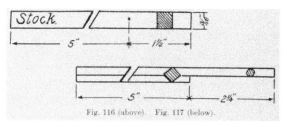

Fig. 116 (above). Fig. 117 (below).

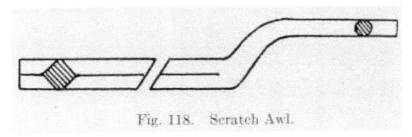

Fig. 118. Scratch Awl.

Fig. 118. Scratch Awl.

Exercise No. 18.—Scratch-Awl.

This tool is used to scratch holes on the surface of metal, and also to lay out shapes on metal. Figure 116 shows the dimensions of stock. The piece should be carbon steel. One and one-half inches from one end, the bar is drawn out until it measures 2¼ inches in length, as shown in Figure 117. It is then bent on an angle as shown in Figure 118. This part is now heated and hammered over the horn of the anvil to form the eye or ring. It is then twisted by catching one end in the vise and twisting to the right. The point is next drawn out as shown in Figure 119. The point is then ground or filed and the awl tempered hard.

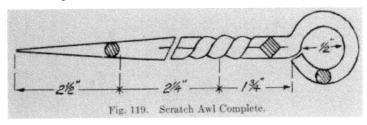

Fig. 119. Scratch Awl Complete.

Fig. 119. Scratch Awl Complete.

Exercise No. 19—Center-Punch.

Figure 120 shows the size of stock and Figure 121 shows the center-punch completed. The top part is first made, then the bottom is drawn out to a taper. In doing this, it is first drawn square, then eight sided and finally rounded. The point is ground and the punch is tempered to a purple color. For heavy centering a larger size steel should be used.

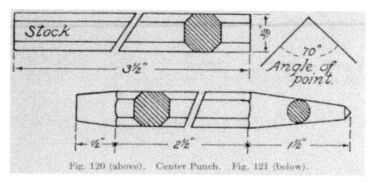

Fig. 120 (above). Center Punch. Fig. 121 (below).

Exercise No. 20—Hand-Punch.

Hand-punches are made of various sizes of stock, ⅝ in., ¾ in. and ⅞ in., and are used for hot punching. Figure 122 shows the size of stock for a punch that will be useful in the school shop, and Figure 123 shows the completed punch. It is made in the same manner as described for the center-punch. This punch must not be tempered. For punching square holes the punch is drawn square, and the ends of all hand-punches are made smaller than the hole to be punched.

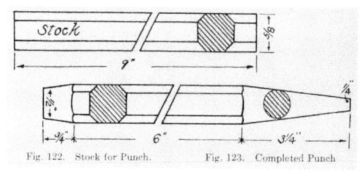

Fig. 122. Stock for Punch. Fig. 123. Completed Punch.

High speed steels, due to their hardness and durability, retain their edge when cutting at extremely high speeds.

It has only been of recent years that high speed steels came into use. Before this time self-hardening steels were made by Jessop and Mushet which were in general use. They were tempered by heating to a dark red and left to cool in the air. The high speed steels of today are heated to 2,000° or 2,200° Fahr., or a white heat bordering on a welding heat.

The chemical composition of these new steels are only known by their makers. However, it is said that they contain carbon, tungsten, chromium, manganese and other elements.

The great advantage in using high speed steel, is that a machine can be run three times as fast as one using carbon steel, without destroying the edge of the tool. The output is therefore greater. Of course, in order to force this steel to do a great amount of work the machine tools should be constructed to stand heavy strains. All kinds of tools are now being made from high speed steel.

For light lathe work, high speed steel is used in the adjustable tool holder. The most common tool for doing heavy work is the round nose which is made from various size steel.

High speed tool steel is sold under many brands. The method of handling is about the same for all. However each manufacturer will give the method which is best for his particular make of steel. In forging high speed lathe tools, a furnace or clean fire with plenty of coke is used. The steel is heated to a bright red heat, holding the steel at this heat as nearly as possible when hammering. Forging at a low heat is liable to cause the steel to burst. When the tool is forged, it is laid in a dry place on the forge to cool. When hardening, the point of the tool is brought to a white welding heat, about 2,100° Fahr., and this is noticeable by the appearance of melted borax, forming on the nose. The tool is now held in a compressed air blast, or dipped into sperm, linseed or lard oil until cool.

Annealing High Speed Steel.

The process is the same as the one used for carbon steel, heating to a red heat and covering the piece with slacked lime until cold.

In cutting high speed tool steel, the bar may be nicked with the emery wheel, then broken.

In working tool steel or iron of any weight the blows of the hammer must be heavy. Light blows stretch the outer part of the metal and not the center. This is liable to fracture it. The blow must be heavy so as to penetrate thru the bar. A trip hammer of ordinary size run by a belt is a very economical tool for the school shop. It is inexpensive and can be used to advantage in drawing out large pieces of stock, especially tool steel.

Every pupil should have more or less practice in the handling of a trip or steam hammer.

II—ART SMITHING

CHAPTER VIII.
Wrought Iron Work—Making a Wrought Iron Leaf—Making a Volute Scroll—Grilles.

At the present time great interest is being taken in the teaching of art work in our public schools. Every school of importance is doing something in the way of giving the pupils a knowledge of art. One working in the school crafts should study art. There is no craft work that one can do well without this training. With art training one can see defects in his work much quicker than without such training. In fact, it opens up a new world of possibilities to the workman. The more one is convinced of the value of thoro acquaintance with the medium in which he is working, the higher the class of work he produces.

All fine workmen in any craft have more or less ability to draw. This not only gives them power to transfer their conceptions to paper, but it also helps them in the execution of the work. The iron-worker in particular should practice free-hand drawing. It enables him to form his material into proper shape. As a general thing, forge work is fashioned into shape by eye.

Fig. 1. Forged Leaf.

Wrought iron-work is one of the oldest of the handicrafts. It was extensively practiced by the ancients and carried to a high degree of excellence, both in execution and design. During the Middle Ages and up to the seventeenth century some of the finest examples were produced. A study of the older forms, especially those of Medieval German production, shows iron fashioned in keeping with its properties and with the spirit of the craftsman. It is impossible to utilize natural forms in wrought iron without convention. Realistic iron flowers are inconsistent with the material in which they are executed. They kill the strength and destroy the character of the metal. This should be learned early by one working in iron. When the iron-worker of the past imitated nature too closely in leaf and flower, he failed as a designer and his work deteriorated. Iron as a crude metal must be fashioned into shapes that are suitable and practical for the material. For instance, it readily allows itself to be worked into graceful curved forms which can be used to advantage in grille work. It may be surface-decorated by using chasing tools. This may be done on hot or cold metal, depending upon the depth wanted. Iron may also be punctured with openings thru the metal which give the play of light and shadow that is very pleasing. Grotesque figures and an endless variety of leaf forms may also be worked in iron. These should be conventionalized. Embossed or repousse work may be done to advantage. In doing this the metal while hot is hammered on the end grain of elm wood and on forms made from iron. When cold it is hammered on lead, and steel tools are used to sharpen up the detail.

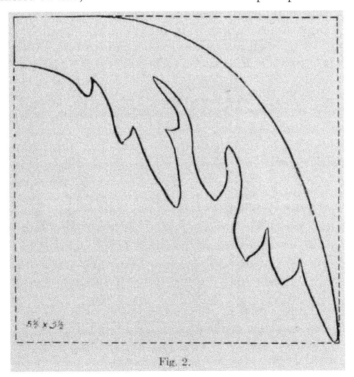

Fig. 2.

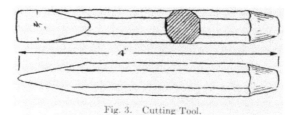

Fig. 3. Cutting Tool.

Fig. 3. Cutting Tool.

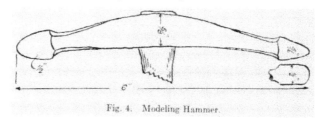

Fig. 4. Modeling Hammer.

Fig. 4. Modeling Hammer.

In Figure 1 is shown a leaf made from Number 16 sheet steel and Figure 2 shows a pattern of the same leaf. In making a leaf of this kind, a full-size drawing is made just as it should look when modeled. From this drawing a pattern is developed as the leaf would look when in the flat. It is impossible to lay it out accurately. The method used is to find the stretch out of the leaf by measuring along its greatest length. This can be done by using a pair of dividers. The length found is then laid off on the metal. The widest parts of the leaf are then measured and laid on the metal. Having the length and width, the rest can be sketched in. The leaf is now cut out with a narrow cold chisel that can be made to follow the curved line. This cutting should be done while the metal is cold. The leaf shown in the illustration has been fluted with a steel hand-tool. In doing this a tool as shown in Figure 3 is used. This tool is made smooth, rounded at the base like an ordinary fuller and then hardened. The fluting is also done while the metal is cold. Lines are marked on the metal with a slate pencil and then sunken with the tool and hammer. In modeling the leaf a hammer like the one shown in Figure 4 is used. It is called the modeling hammer. This hammer has a ball on one end and a pein on the other, both of which are made very smooth and without sharp corners. These hammers are made in various sizes. In modelling the leaf it is heated and hammered on the back side with the ball of the hammer, using the elm block to hammer on. The ends of the lobes are then formed to give the whole a decorative effect. These leaves are generally used in grille work and are welded into position. In Figure 5 is shown part of a grille with a similar leaf welded on. In welding leaves to the members of grille work the bottom part of the leaf is formed around the bar; caught with a pair of tongs, it is heated, using a flux when hot. It is then taken to the anvil and welded. A small collar is finally welded in front of the leaf as shown in the illustration.

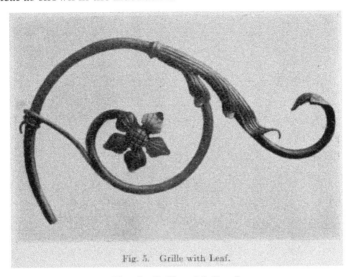

Fig. 5. Grille with Leaf.

The leaves shown in the illustrations are made to cover the grille on but one side. If a grille is to be seen from both sides when in place, the leaves are cut out symmetrically and then bent and modeled to fit over the top and sides of the bars so that they appear finished from both sides. Figure 6 shows the pattern of such a leaf.

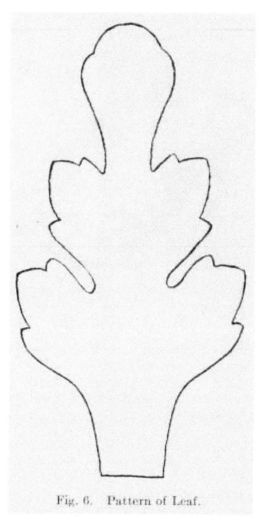

Fig. 6. Pattern of Leaf.

Fig. 6. Pattern of Leaf.

The following exercises will be of a simple nature to give the beginner an idea of the tools and processes used in producing this kind of work by hand. The writer does not claim that the following method is the only one to be used in doing this work. There are many other ways to execute these exercises and one should use his own ingenuity in designing and executing individual pieces. It is hoped that pupils will be encouraged to originate designs of their own to work out in this interesting metal.

The tools used in making these exercises will be the ordinary forge shop tools that can be made, and will be described later on, as they are needed.

Exercise No. 1.

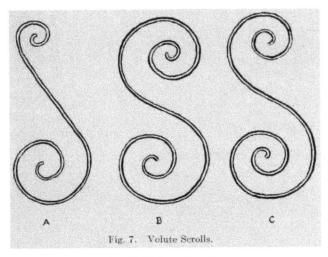

Fig. 7. Volute Scrolls.

Fig. 7. Volute Scrolls.

Volute Scroll. This exercise is given in order to familiarize one with the bending of curved forms and also to train the hand and eye in doing free-hand work. No metal lends itself more readily to the bending of curves than wrought iron. The scroll is an important element in the designing of iron doors, window grilles, etc. In bending, the scroll must not have kinks or flat places, but a gradual curve. If it is desired to suggest strength, the scroll is coiled tightly; or if lightness of effect is desired, it is coiled loosely. In making a scroll to fit some particular place a drawing is made with chalk on a surface plate. The scroll is then measured along the line with a string to find its length. In Figure 7 are shown drawings of typical scrolls. The one at A shows too much space between the coils. The scroll at B is top-heavy owing to the coils being equal in size. The one at C has a continuous curve with unequal coils which balance better. In bending a scroll from a flat piece of stock, as shown in Figure 8, the end is heated and hammered on the corners to make it round at one end. It is then bent over the outer edge of the anvil, as shown in Figure 9 A and B, to form the eye. It is then heated for a considerable part of its length and rolled up as shown at C. If any kinks get into the bar they can be rectified by hammering on the horn. This is the method used in forming a scroll with the hammer. In heating the bar to be rolled into scroll form, it must not be heated to a white heat. Scrolls are also bent over forms when a great number are wanted. Heavy scrolls are formed by bending in a bending fork that fits into a square hole in the anvil. (See fork in Figure 10.) A monkey wrench is used to bend the bar when in the fork.

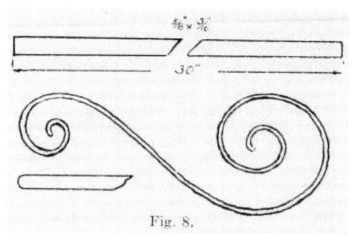

Fig. 8.

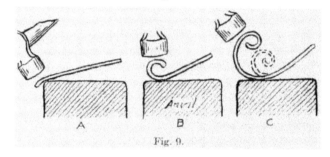

Fig. 9.

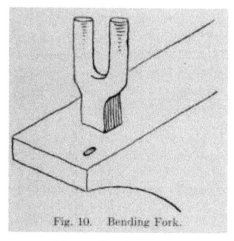

Fig. 10. Bending Fork.

In Figure 11 and Figure 12 are shown grilles which are made from flat stock. The scrolls in this case were made after the bars had been welded in place. They could be made first and then riveted or fastened with iron bands, but welding of course makes a better job.

Fig. 11. Grille.

In Figure 13 is shown a drawing for a welded scroll. Notice the dotted line at A. This is where the weld is made. At B, the pieces are shown in position to be welded by the separate heat method. In doing this the length is measured on the drawing with a string, and the three pieces cut. The two short ones are upset; and one is laid on top of the other; then heated and welded at the same time they are scarfed. The long piece is upset and welded to the short one. They are then formed.

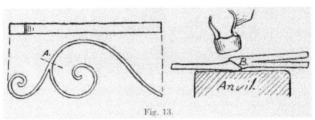

Fig. 13.

Fig. 12. Grille.

CHAPTER IX.

Twisting—Braiding—Making a Fire Shovel.

Exercise No. 2.

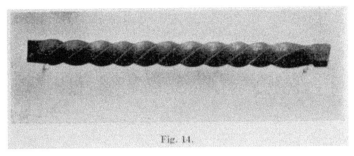

Fig. 14.

Twisting. A piece of one-half inch square stock, nine inches long, is heated its entire length, one end caught in a vise and with a monkey wrench or heavy pair of tongs on the other, it is twisted to the right. If the heat is an even one and not too hot, the spacing of the twist will be uniform. In case one part twists faster than another, a little water is used to cool that part. The beauty of twisted work depends on having the spacing uniform between the turns. (See Figure 14.) Flat stock can also be twisted in this manner. To straighten twisted work, it is heated red, set on the end grain of elm wood and hammered with a wooden mallet. The mallet used in this work should be made from hickory. For heavy striking a little band of iron can be put on the mallet a half-inch from one end, so that the mallet will not split. The block on which to straighten the iron should be about ten inches in diameter and three feet high. A short block about eight inches wide and twelve inches long may be set into the coal box, having coal under and around it to hold it in place. This makes a very handy block on which to bump up light pieces of metal or to straighten metal.

Exercise No. 3.

Figure 15 shows the dimensions of stock for a twisted poker-handle. The four ¼-inch rods are upset on one end until they measure six inches. They are then welded together on this end. This is done by first twisting a strong binding wire around the rods to keep them in place while taking the heat. (See Figure 16.) In welding, they are welded directly on the ends and scarfed as shown in Figure 15.

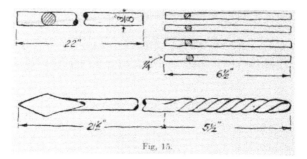

Fig. 15.

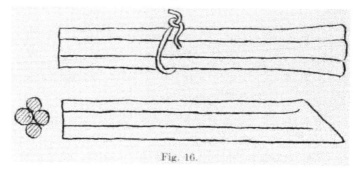

Fig. 16.

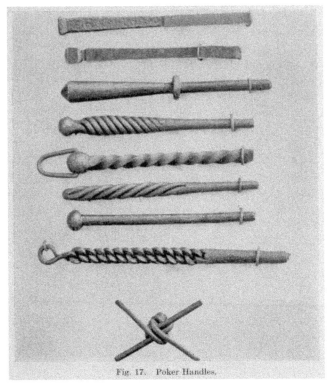

Fig. 17. Poker Handles.

Notice that the scarf is made so that the point of the scarf on the other piece will come onto a one-quarter inch rod and not between the two. The scarf must not be hammered farther back from the ends than ³⁄₈-inch. The ³⁄₈-inch bar is now upset on one end and scarfed. The two parts are then welded, smoothing the weld with the hand hammer. The end of the handle is welded directly at the ends of the rods. The entire handle is heated uniformly, caught in a vise and twisted to the right. If any part twists faster than another, that part is cooled with water dropped from a hole in the bottom of a tin cup. In twisting the handle, the ³⁄₈ bar is caught in the vise. A strong pair of tongs are used on the end of the handle to twist it, or the end of the handle can be caught with a monkey wrench. The point of the poker is drawn to a square point and then flattened. In making pokers or shovels, the stock may be either round or square. In Figure 17 are shown some handles that are suitable for pokers or shovels. A method of braiding the last handle shown in the illustration is to weld four ³⁄₁₆-in. rods of either round or square stock to a piece of ½-inch round stock. Two of the rods are then bent over at right angles to the one-half inch piece. The others are bent over them, and so on until finished. The four rods are then welded at the top and a ring turned. The last illustration shows the method of bending the rods.

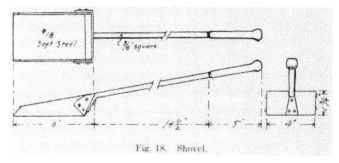

Fig. 18. Shovel.

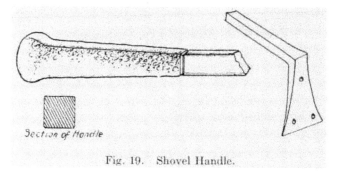

Fig. 19. Shovel Handle.

Exercise No. 4.

Shovel.—Figure 18 shows the dimensions and form of the exercise. In making the handle, ⅜-in. square stock is used. The piece is cut 25 inches long. On one end the piece is upset considerably in order to get a good sized head. Five inches from the end of the head a line is cut on four sides with a chisel. This part is then hammered with a ball hammer while hot to give it a rough texture as shown in Figure 19. The other end of the handle is upset a little, bent on an angle and flattened, letting it get as wide as it will.

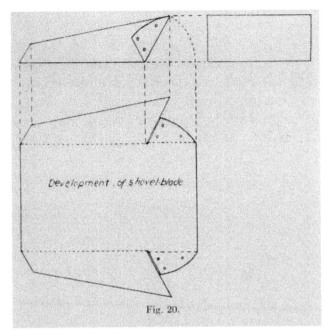

Fig. 20.

The development of the pattern for the shovel blade is shown in Figure 20. At the top is shown a side and end elevation of the shovel. The dimensions should be drawn full size. The shapes of the sides and of the ends are found by measuring from the elevation. The pattern should be made from sheet iron and kept for future use.

In forming the shovel, the sides are first bent up by using the vise and heel of the anvil. This forming must be done while the metal is cold. The end of the shovel may be bent by hammering it over a heavy, flat piece of iron. The corners are hammered around the sides by catching the shovel in the vise. They are fastened by drilling holes thru both pieces and riveting them, using a rivet set to finish the rivets. In fastening the handle to the blade or shovel, three Number 10 round-head rivets are used. If desired, the handle can be made from larger stock, also increasing the size and the thickness of the shovel.

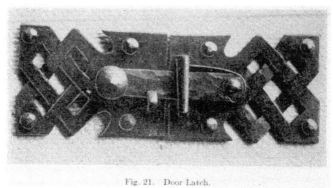

Fig. 21. Door Latch.

- 84 -

CHAPTER X.

Making a Door-latch—Making a Hinge—Making a Candle-stick.

Exercise No. 5.

Door latch.—In Figure 21 is shown a latch for a double door. In Figure 22 are shown the dimensions of the two plates and the bar latch. In making the plates, a piece of soft steel, 2 in. wide and ⅛-in. thick is used. The design is sketched on the metal and five $\frac{9}{32}$-in. holes are drilled in each plate where the square holes come in the design. The plates are then heated and a square punch is used to drift out the holes. The outside edges are then cut. The plate is heated and with a square punch the metal is set down to give it the interlaced effect as shown in Figure 23.

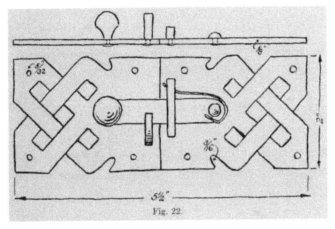

Fig. 22.

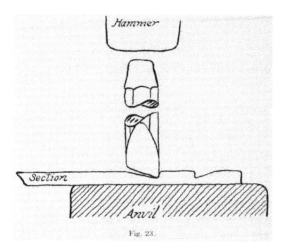

Fig. 23.

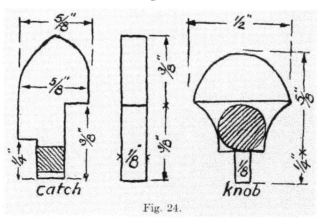

Fig. 24.

The plates are now filed to straighten the square holes, and the holes on the corners for screws are drilled. Figure 24 represents the catch, which can be made as shown, and the knob which is worked out on the end of a rod, as shown in Figure 25. It is hammered on the outer edge of the anvil. After each blow it is turned until finished. Then it is cut off and the tenon is filed. The guard shown in Figure 26 is cut from a flat piece as represented. The bar is made from ½ by ³⁄₁₆-in. stock, drilled, and a slot is sawed for the spring. The spring is about ⅛ by ³⁄₃₂-in. and can be made from spring steel.

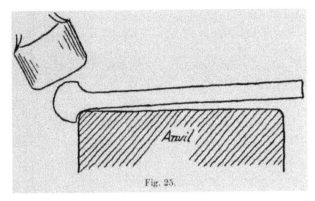

Fig. 25.

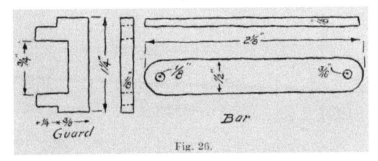

Fig. 26.

Figure 27 represents a hinge that can be made from ⅛-in. soft steel. After the design is sketched with a slate pencil on the metal, the open parts are drilled and cut out. The outside is next cut with a chisel and the edges are filed smooth. The eye or joint of the hinge is formed without welding, by hammering it around an eye pin of the desired size. The prongs or projections to form the knuckle are filed so that they fit into one another. The interlacing is done with a square end punch in the same manner as explained for the latch. A great variety of designs of this kind can be made to advantage in iron. A drawing of a simple strap hinge is shown in Figure 28. The part of the strap at A on the drawing is made greater in length than width for appearance. This gives the strap apparent strength and emphasizes its length.

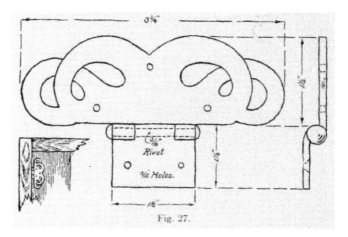

Fig. 27.

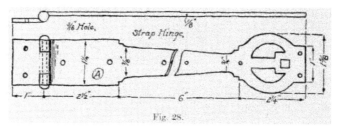

Fig. 28.

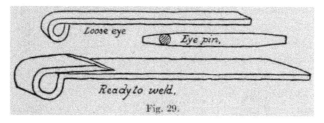

Fig. 29.

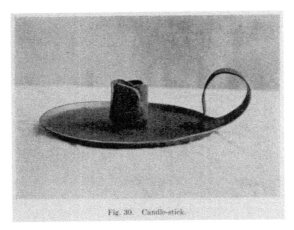

Fig. 30. Candle-stick.

The hinge can be made any length desired but should be carefully proportioned; the eye can be made loose or welded. In welding a hinge-eye the lap should always be on the back. Note the drawing of the eye ready for welding in Figure 29. In making hinges, the making of the eye is always the first operation. A welded eye makes the strongest hinge; but it can be made with a loose eye if desired. In bending and finishing the eye, an eye-pin should be used to true the hole. An eye-pin is a piece of round steel of the desired size drawn tapering on each end so that it can be driven thru a hole. The projections that form the joint for a loose eye hinge should be cut out before the eye is made. If the stock is light, the joint in either a loose or a welded hinge can be filed or sawed after the eye is turned. In a heavy eye the projections are laid off and marked on the metal while flat. The bar is then heated and split lengthwise from one side, starting ½-inch from the end, and cutting long enough to make the eye. The eye is then formed and welded, and pieces are cut out leaving alternating projections which can be filed to fit.

Exercise No. 6.

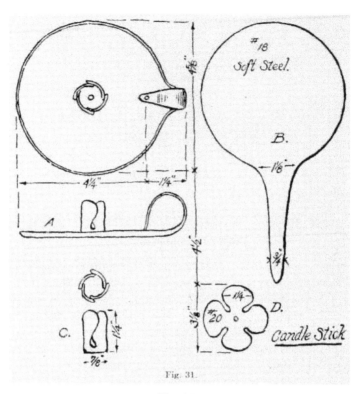

Fig. 31.

Exercise No. 6 is a candle-stick. The reproduction, Figure 30, shows the finished piece. The drawing, Figure 31, at A, gives the dimensions; at B, is shown the pattern of the bottom in the flat. The bottom is cut from a sheet of soft steel, using a narrow cold chisel. The edge is then filed and bent up about one-quarter of an inch. In doing so, it is hammered over a round block or iron which fits into the square hole of the anvil. See Figure 32. The handle is formed by heating it, and hammering it over the horn of the anvil. In making the socket to hold the candle as shown at C, Figure 31, the piece is cut from number 20 soft steel. At D, is illustrated the stock cut ready for forming.

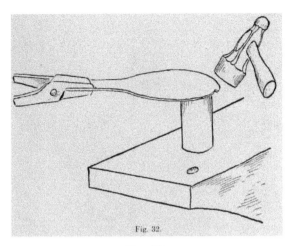

Fig. 32.

In cutting this piece, the shape is sketched with a slate pencil on the metal. Five holes are now drilled, the center hole, $^5/_{32}$ in. in diameter and four $^3/_{16}$-in. holes at the base of leaves. A narrow cold chisel is then used which will cut on a curved line. The edges of the pieces are then filed; the piece is heated and hammered on the elm block to raise it. In raising the socket, it is heated in the center, set over a depression in the block and hammered. This brings the wings or leaves up. They are brought up until they overlap one another, the leaves forming a square box. The whole piece is then heated, placed on the end of a $^3/_4$-in. round bar, setting the whole into a swage, and the leaves are fitted around the bar by hammering. The socket is then riveted in place. A rivet is put in the end of the handle to hold it in place. The candle-stick is now smoothed with a file and smoked over the fire, then oiled.

Wrought Iron Lantern.

CHAPTER XI.

Making a Drawer Pull—Chasing—Making a Door-knocker— Repousse—Perforated Decoration.

Exercise No. 7.

Drawer pulls can be of one part, the handle being fastened directly to the drawer, or they may be of two parts, the handle and plate. The handle can be made stationary on the plate or movable. In Figure 33 are shown some hinges, drawer pulls and key escutcheons. The open work is cut out while the stock is hot, or if light stock is used, it may be drilled, cut and filed while the plate is cold.

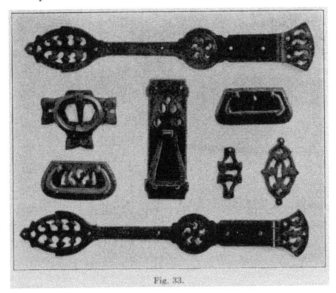

Fig. 33.

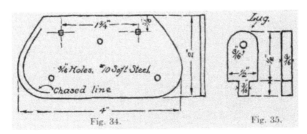

Fig. 34. Fig. 35.

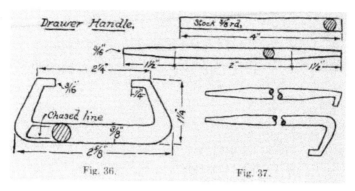

Fig. 36. Fig. 37.

The stock used in making a plate for a pull, somewhat like those illustrated, is represented in Figure 34. After the plate is cut to size, which is done cold with a hand chisel, the outside surface is hammered while hot with a ball hammer, drawing the plate a little thinner near the edge. This hammering gives the surface a rough texture. The edges are now ground or filed to shape and the holes are drilled as shown in the drawing. The round holes are for screws to fasten the pull, and the square holes are to fasten lugs, on which the handle is to swing. The lugs are shown in Figure 35. The tenon can be filed, the top rounded, the holes drilled, and the lugs riveted into the plate. When riveting the lugs, they are caught in a vise, the plate set on and the tenons are riveted tight into the holes. The square holes in the plate should be countersunk a little on the back before the lugs are riveted.

The handle is a movable one, and the drawing is shown in Figure 36. The different steps in making the handle are represented in Figure 37. When the stock, which should be soft steel, is cut, the ends are heated and drawn out tapering to $3/16$ inch at the end. One-and-a-half inches from each end of the bar is marked with a center punch. The ends are now bent over $1/4$ inch, then the bar is bent at the center marks. When the handle is formed to fit the plate it is smoothed with a file. If desired, a line can be chased on the handle and around the edge of plate. In doing this a short, light chisel is used. After lines are traced on the plate with a slate pencil the chisel is set on the line and struck with a light hammer; at the same time it is drawn towards the worker with the lead corner of the cutting edge directly on and above the line.

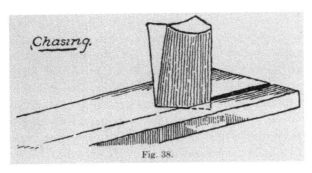

Fig. 38.

The chisel should receive rapid, light blows and be continually moved toward the workman. The lead corner of the chisel should be guided onto the line while the other corner is doing the cutting. See Figure 38, a rather large sized drawing of the cutting edge of the chisel. When the lines are chased with the chisel, they should be gone over again with quite hard blows of the hammer, forcing the chisel down to make the lines quite pronounced.

To put the handle in place on the plate, it is heated and sprung into the holes of the lugs. The last thing to do in finishing all work of this kind is to heat it to a dark red. All scale and dirt is then scraped off; when cool, some oil is put on. For this kind of work, machine oil is good. The reason it is heated to a dark, even red heat is that when cool the handle and the plate will have the same color and texture.

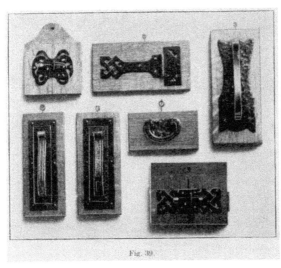

Fig. 39.

Exercise No. 8.

In Figure 39 are shown some hinges, latches and door knockers. Figure 40 is a drawing of a simple knocker. The plate is cut out and the line around the edge is chased with a tool. The chasing tool is simply a cold chisel ground to a short bevel and rounded somewhat like a fuller, as shown in Figure 41. A short chisel is used for cold work and a longer one for hot work. The chasing can be done while the metal is cold. If it is to be very deep or wide the plate is heated and a longer chisel is used. The lug at Figure 42 is made and riveted into the plate. The top of the hammer is filed to straddle it. A hole is then drilled and a rivet put thru. Holes are drilled around the edge of the plate for screws or nails.

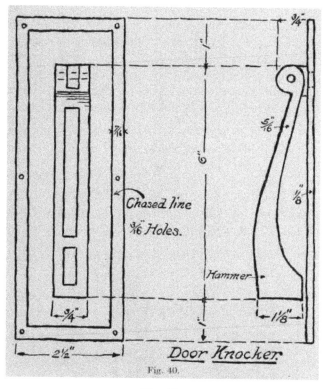

Fig. 40.

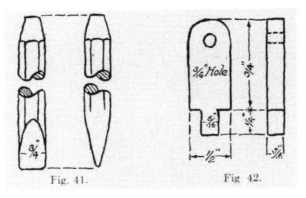

Fig. 41. Fig. 42.

In making the hammer a piece of ¾-inch square, soft steel is used. It is upset on one end to get the stock large enough for the bottom of the hammer. The bar is then drawn out on the horn as shown at Figure 43. The top part is formed as shown at Figure 44. Lines are chased on the front of hammer as shown in the drawing; this can be done after it is formed. If the lines are to be very deep it should be done while the piece is straight and heated.

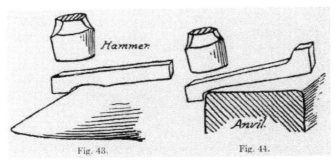

Fig. 43. Fig. 44.

There is ample room for design in the making of door knockers, both for outside and inside doors of dwellings. Knocker plates for doors on the inside of dwellings can be elaborated by a combination of repousse, chasing and perforated decoration which give a variety of light and shadow. Perforated plates can be backed up with colored leather or cloth which gives a very pleasing contrast to the metal.

Fig. 45.

In Figure 45 is shown an interior door knocker. It is backed up with colored leather. The plates are made of ⅛-in. thick, soft steel. After the plates are cut out, the openings are marked with a slate pencil and gone over with a short cold chisel to mark them. The plate is then heated, and the part enclosed by the chisel line is cut out. A very narrow chisel, 12 in. long, is used to do the cutting. The cutting is all done from the outside. This gives the edge a slight bevel. The edges of open places are trued up with a file. The openings must not be filed too exact and smooth. The most essential thing to look after is form; the work looks best when it shows handwork and is not mechanical.

Fig. 46.

Fig. 46.

Handwork is most in keeping with the design and the material. The lines on the plate are chased with a narrow chisel and the foliated form bumped out from the back by hammering on the end grain of the elm block. The hammer that does the knocking is hinged on the top plate so that the bottom part moves out and in when knocking. Very thin red leather is glued on the back of the plate with fish glue. The diameter of the top plate is 4½-in., the bottom 2½-in., and the hammer is 6¾-in. long.

A good method of working out ideas for pieces of this character is to make numerous rough sketches on paper with a lead pencil, making one line over another without erasing. When one gets what he thinks is good it is redrawn and perfected. It may then be worked in the material.

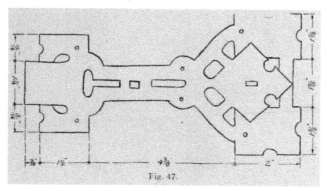
Fig. 47.

Fig. 47.

At Figure 46 is shown a door knocker hinged at the top. The plate is one piece. At Figure 47 are shown the dimensions of the plate. After the shape of the plate is sketched on the metal, the lines are traced with a chisel. The open work is then cut out, and the outside of the plate is cut and filed. The center leaf at the top of the plate is indicated by forcing the metal down along the top edge of the leaf with a punch, also at the bottom to form the interlace. The plate should be hot when this is done. The hammer shown in Figure 48 should be forged from ¾-in. square, soft steel. The lug shown on the drawing is to be made and riveted into the top of the plate. The hammer is then placed over the lug, and the lug is drilled to conform to the drilled holes in the hammer.

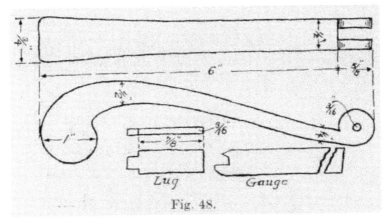

Fig. 48.

Fig. 48.

The chasing on the plate and hammer is done with a chisel as previously explained. A gauge should be made from a piece of steel to scratch the guide lines on the plate for the chasing as shown in Figure 48. These lines are then cut with the chisel.

CHAPTER XII.

Making a Hat and Coat Hook—A Fuller—Jump Welding—Making a Wall Hook.

Exercise No. 9.

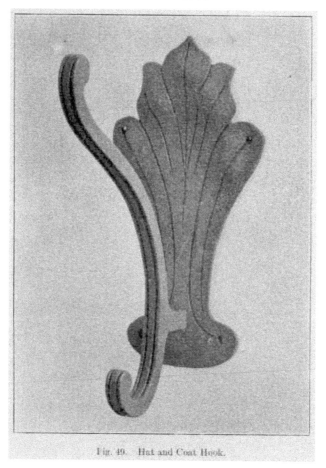

Fig. 49. Hat and Coat Hook.

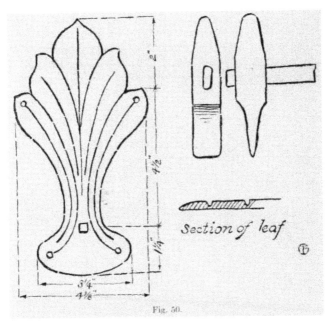

Section of leaf

Fig. 50.

Fig. 50.

Figure 49 represents a hat-and-coat hook. In the making of this piece, the plate should be made from No. 14 soft steel. The dimensions are shown in Figure 50. The shape of the plate can be drawn on heavy paper, which is afterward cut out and used as a pattern when making the plate from metal. After the plate is cut out with a cold chisel, it is ground or filed on the edges. The holes are next drilled, and the lines are cut on the surface as shown in the drawing. In cutting the lines, a short, narrow cold chisel is used for chasing in the same manner as previously described. The lines on the leaf should be made quite deep. A fuller is shown in Figure 50, which is used to make the lines still deeper. The fuller should have the edge smooth, and without sharp corners. The plate should be clamped on to a surface plate while making the lines. The fuller is then set on the cut lines and struck with the hand hammer, chasing the tool to the ends of the lines. This work can, also, be done to advantage by heating the plate and having a helper hold it on the anvil while fullering the lines. When all the lines are made, the leaf is heated, set on the elm block and hammered on the back to raise the end of the lobes as shown in the illustration.

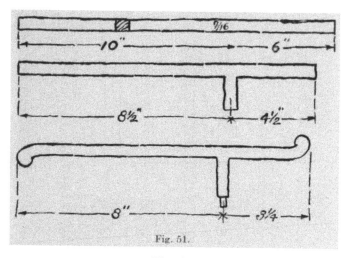

Fig. 51.

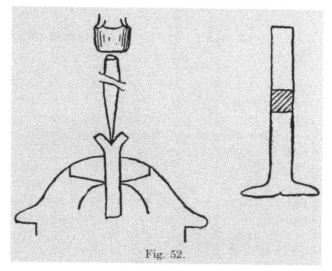

Fig. 52.

Fig. 53.

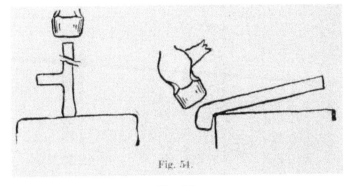

Fig. 54.

The hook is made from iron. Figure 51 represents the dimensions of stock for the hook. The lug is welded on, and the ends of the bar are rounded ready to be formed. After the stock is cut, it is upset six inches from one end to enlarge it so that the lug can be welded on. The stock from which the lug is made is cut 3½ inches long, upset on end, and split in the vise ½ inch deep as shown at Figure 52. The split end should be formed as shown. In welding, separate heats are taken, and the lug is jumped onto the bar as shown in Figure 53. The first blows are struck directly on the end of the lug, then the lips are welded. Figure 51 shows the length of the piece before the knobs are formed. In making the knobs at the end, they should be upset as shown in Figure 54. They are then hammered as shown, and finally rounded. The lug is next cut the proper length, and a shoulder is filed at the end. The chased lines are now cut on the front side. In forming the piece, it is heated and hammered over the horn of the anvil, starting to bend at the end first, and working toward the center. In bending anything of this kind, always start at one end, and finish as you work toward the other end. See the drawing of the bent hook at Figure 55. The end of the lug is next heated and caught in a vise, the plate is set on and riveted tightly. The work is smoothed with a file, heated to darken it, and oiled.

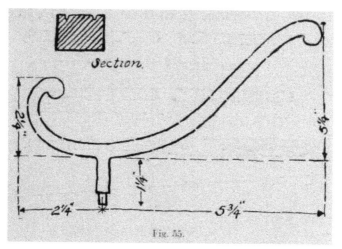

Fig. 55.

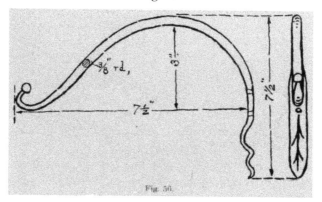

Fig. 56.

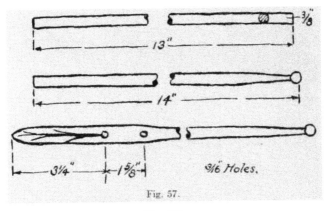

Fig. 57.

Exercise No. 10.

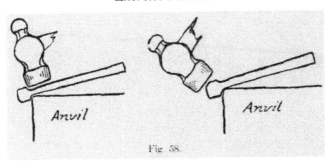

Fig. 58.

A wall hook, suitable to hang a bird cage or fern dish, is shown in Figure 56. In Figure 57 are shown the length and size of stock, and the piece ready to form. In making the ball, the piece is shouldered at one end by hammering it on the outer edge of the anvil as shown in Figure 58. It is then hammered on the corner, to make it round. The other end is drawn to a square point, and is then flattened as shown in Figure 59, letting it become as wide as it will. This flat end is then veined suggesting a leaf form. In doing this, a long chisel, made round somewhat like a fuller, is used. The piece is heated, and a sunken line is made with the chisel, as shown by the drawing of the leaf end. The piece is then heated, and the leaf end is formed. The holes should now be drilled. The balance of the hook is heated and formed by hammering it over the horn of the anvil.

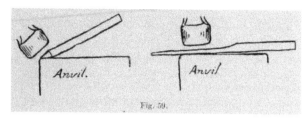

Fig. 59.

Hall Lanterns.

CHAPTER XIII.
Making a Toasting-fork—Inlaying.

Exercise No. 11.

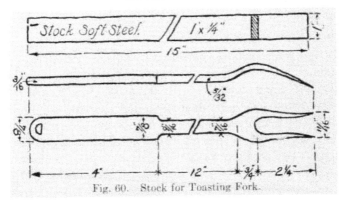

Fig. 60. Stock for Toasting Fork.

A very interesting and useful article to make is a toasting fork. The stock used can be spring steel. A disadvantage in using this steel is that it is too hard to work out a design on the handle. If one can weld quite well, the fork should have the handle made of soft steel and the balance of carbon steel. In doing this, the weld is the first thing to do while the stock is straight and full size. If one without much welding experience is to make the fork, it should be made of soft steel, and when finished the prongs should be case hardened. In making a fork of this kind, a piece of soft steel as shown in the drawing in Figure 60 is used. On one end, the stock is enlarged a little, by upsetting for a distance of five or six inches. This end is to be used for the handle. The other end of the bar is then heated, and a hole is punched 1¾-in. from the end. The piece should then look somewhat like the drawing at A, Figure 61. In drawing out, the shoulder is hammered as shown at B, Figure 61. The shank (the part between the handle and the shoulder) is next drawn out. It should be a scant ¼-in. thick so as to finish to the dimensions given in Figure 60. Care must be taken to avoid getting too much stock in the shank. It is a very easy matter to get too much stock between the handle and the shoulder which, when drawn out, is too long. The prongs are roughly made by cutting the stock out as shown by the dotted lines in Figure 61. When this is done the prongs are hammered out to the correct size, allowing for finishing.

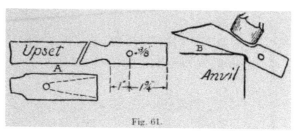

Fig. 61.

In Figure 62 are shown reproductions of similar forks. The line shown running around the rectangular open parts is inlaid copper. A channel is sunken and the copper driven into it. In making the handle, the three oblong holes are punched while hot with a punch about $\frac{3}{16}$ in. by $\frac{5}{8}$ in. at the end, making a series of punchings to cut out the holes. The holes should be small enough so that they may be finished to size with a file. Notice that the openings are not of the same size; but two short ones, with a longer one in the center, give variety. Notice, also, that the shape of the handle is in keeping with the long, slim shank and the slender, two-tine fork at the end.

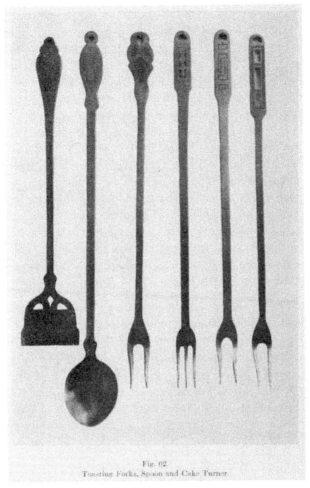

Fig. 62. Toasting Forks, Spoon and Cake Turner.

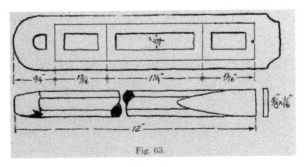

Fig. 63.

After the handle is shaped, and the holes are punched, including the one at the top to hang the fork by, the line to receive the copper is marked. (See Figure 63.) The marking should be done with a scratch awl. The line is then cut with a small chisel. This cutting should be quite deep and exact. This is important if the work is to be true and straight. All of the marking should be done while the handle is cold. It is now heated and taken to the anvil. A small punch, as represented in Figure 63, is then set onto the cut line and given a blow with the hammer, sinking the punch about $\frac{1}{16}$ of an inch. One-half of the punch is now raised up and out of the channel. While it is directly on the chased line, it is given another blow with the hammer and so on until the end is reached. The particular thing to watch is to have the lead corner of punch directly on the chased guide line, while the other edge of the punch is in the channel in order to keep the finished line straight. Keep the punch in good order, straight and square at the end. The punch should not have much taper and should not be used after the red heat leaves the metal. After the entire line has been sunken $\frac{1}{16}$ in. deep, the handle is reheated and the line is sunken perhaps $\frac{1}{8}$ in. deep.

A wider punch is now used in the long channel to straighten it and make it deeper. The wide punch should have no taper and should be a scant $\frac{3}{32}$ in. thick so that the line will be about $\frac{3}{32}$ in. wide. If any part of the channel should be too wide, the handle should be hammered on the edge with a light hammer to close the channel a little. When the channel is finished, the handle should be filed flat on the channel side. This will give one a better view of the straightness of the channel.

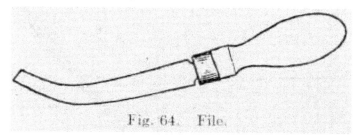

Fig. 64. File.

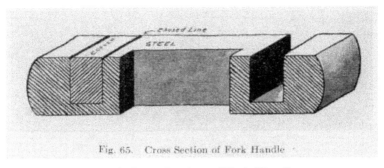

Fig. 65. Cross Section of Fork Handle

Fig. 65. Cross Section of Fork Handle.

In case the channel is not as straight as it should be, a small flat file is heated and bent at the end and rehardened. (See Figure 64.) This file is used to straighten up the edges of the channel. A small cold chisel can also be used for this purpose. The channel must be straight along the top edge. When the channel is well straightened, strips of copper are filed to fit the channel, letting them project above the channel about $\frac{3}{32}$ of an inch and also having each piece a little short in length. When the pieces are all in place, the handle is set on the anvil and with a heavy hammer they are driven down forcing the copper to fill the whole of the channel. The entire handle is filed to the dimensions given in Figure 63.

Notice Figure 65 which shows a sectional drawing of the handle, with the copper in place and a chased line running along between copper and steel. A channel without copper is shown at the right of the illustration.

Wrought Iron Lamp.

CHAPTER XIV.

Making a Lantern—Making a Wall-lamp.

Exercise No. 12.

Fig. 66. Lantern.

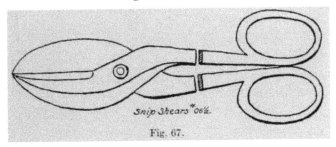

Fig. 67.

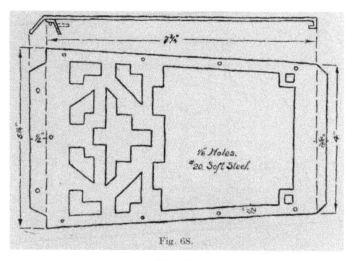

Fig. 68.

The lantern shown in Figure 66 consists of four sides which are fastened together with angles and rivets. The top is made from four pieces, with angles also riveted to them. The stock is cut with a pair of snip shears, No. 06½. (See Figure 67.) The sides must be cut to the same size or there will be trouble in putting them together. After they are cut, the open work is marked with a slate pencil. Holes are drilled in the corners of each opening, and they are cut out with a sharp chisel. The edges are filed and all holes are drilled for No. 12 rivets. At Figure 68 is a drawing, with dimensions of one of the sides as it should be in the flat. Notice the section of the sheet bent at the top for the roof and at the bottom to hold the glass. The glass is held in position at the top with a little strip of copper, with a rivet to hold it. The glass is set into the groove at the bottom, and the copper cleat is bent over the top of the glass. The copper cleat should be ⅞ by ⅜ in., made from No. 26 soft copper. The bottom of the sheet is first bent at right angles, then a flat piece ³⁄₁₆ in. thick is laid on the inside of the sheet, and the whole is placed on the anvil. The end of the sheet is now hammered over the ³⁄₁₆-in. piece with a mallet to make the pocket to hold the glass. All of the holes for rivets to fasten the angles should be countersunk a little on the inside. The angles are made from one inch wide No. 20 hoop iron. They are formed by placing them between two pieces of flat iron as shown in Figure 69, and holding the whole in a vise while hammering with a wood mallet.

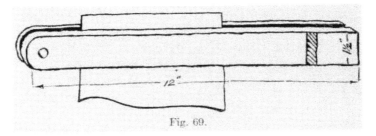

Fig. 69.

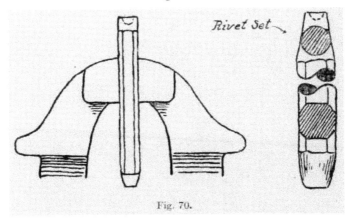

Fig. 70.

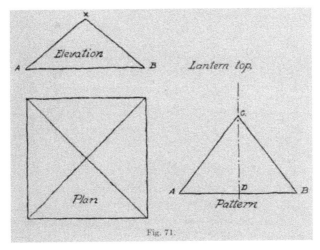

Fig. 71.

In fastening the angles to the sides, the heads of the rivets are on the outside, and the inside is smooth. In doing this, the heads of the rivets are held in a rivet set while hammering on the inside.

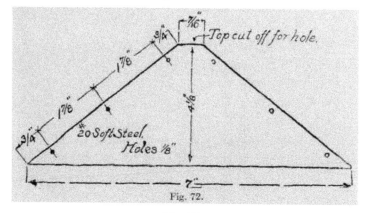

Fig. 72.

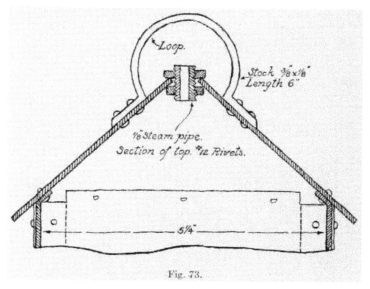

Fig. 73.

The rivet set is caught in a vise as shown in Figure 70. A rivet set is a piece of steel with the shape of a rivet head sunken into one end. In making this, a punch is filed the shape of a rivet head and is then driven into the end of a hot piece of steel. In Figure 71 is shown a simple method of developing a pattern of one section for the top of a lantern. A-B of the pattern is first drawn. The length of X-B of the elevation is the length of C-D of the pattern. Lines are then drawn from C to A and B. The point of each section at the top is cut off so that when the four pieces are riveted to the angles there will be a $^7/_{16}$-in. hole thru the top. (See Figure 72.) In this hole is put a piece of $^1/_8$-in. steam pipe with a lock nut on the top and another on the bottom to hold it in place. (See Figure 73.) The pipe is for the socket to screw onto under the top, and also for the wire to come thru. The loop at the top is to suspend the lantern by. It is made of $^3/_8$ by $^1/_8$-in. stock, 6 inches long. Two No. 10 rivets are put in each end to fasten it to the roof. The lamp is to hang by a chain suspended from the ceiling. In doing this a ceiling cap is necessary. This may be a piece of $^1/_2$-in. steam pipe threaded on one end and a hook made on the other. (See drawing, Figure 74.) A cast iron piece is screwed on the end of the pipe and is then fastened to the ceiling by three screws, which supports the chain and lamp. The wires go thru the pipe and connect with other wires in the ceiling. (See drawing of the casting, Figure 75.) When the lamp is wired and the casting is fastened to the ceiling, it must be covered with something to hide the wires and its rough appearance. In Figure 76 is shown a drawing for a cap to cover the casting and wiring. The cap has a hole in the center for the pipe to pass thru, leaving it movable on the pipe. A collar of cast iron, with a set screw in the side, is to go under the cap and the screw tightened when the cap is against the ceiling. (See drawing of the collar, Figure 77.) In making the cap, it is heated and hammered over a hole in the swage block. A hammer with a large-sized, rounded face is used. The disk is driven into the hole until it becomes bowl-shaped and the right height.

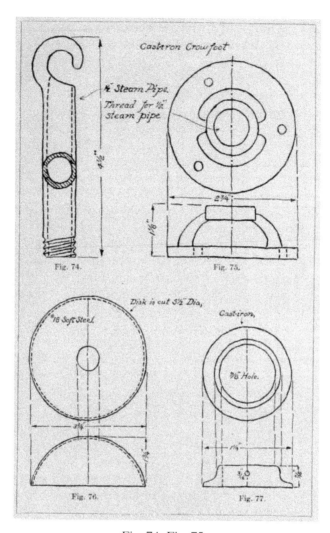

Fig. 74. Fig. 75.

Fig. 76. Fig. 77.

Fig. 78.

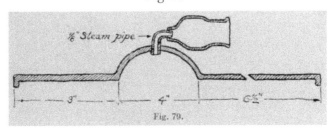

Fig. 79.

At Figure 78 is represented a lamp that is to be fastened to the side of the wall, instead of hanging from the ceiling with a chain. The light is inverted, the lamp being open at the top and closed at the bottom.

The stock used in the construction of the lamp is very heavy, No. 14 soft steel being used. The angle plates on the corners are made from No. 20 soft steel. The plate that is on the back of the lamp has a cup-shaped pocket hammered into it to cover the wiring when the lamp is in place, and on which the light socket is fastened.

In Figure 79 is shown a cross-section of the back plate, with the depression and socket in place.

This kind of lamp is very simple to make and can be made in various shapes and sizes. The back of the lamp can be made of wood instead of metal, if desired.

Wrought Iron Table Lamps.

CHAPTER XV.
Making a Portable Lamp.

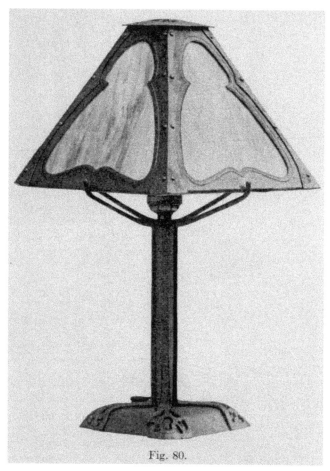

Fig. 80.

In Figure 80 is represented a portable lamp. This kind of lamp can be made in various sizes with one light. The lamp shown in the illustration, consists of two parts; the standard, and the shade, which can be removed. The standard consists of a box-shaped bottom, with a pipe screwed into it for the upright piece. The arms that the shade rests on, are separate and are held in position by the lamp socket, which is screwed down on them. The strips running over the bottom of the base and up the pipe are riveted in place to support the pipe. This gives the whole standard a more substantial appearance, and relieves the plain round pipe.

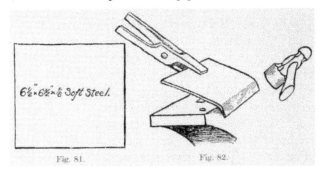

Fig. 81. Fig. 82.

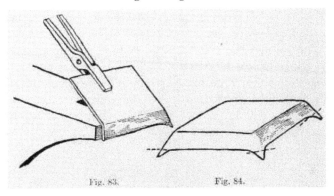

Fig. 83. Fig. 84.

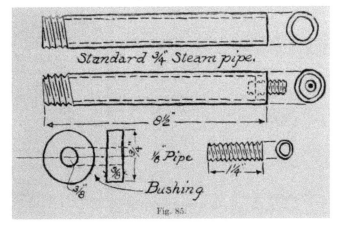

Fig. 85.

In making a very simple lamp of this character, we may eliminate the strips running up the pipe, and make the bottom with a round pipe screwed into it. Of course a square standard would be more in keeping with the square base and shade. In making the box-shaped base, soft steel should be used. Figure 81 shows the dimensions of the flat stock. The plate is heated and an inch of the edge is bent over the outer edge of the anvil, as shown in Figure 82. The outer edges of the plate can be bent over the end of the anvil as shown in Figure 83. When all the edges are bent the piece will look somewhat as in Figure 84. The corners are now ground off, and the bottom is made level. A hole is drilled in the center and threaded for a ¾-in. steam pipe. Two inches from the center hole, another hole is drilled and tapped for a ¼-in. or ⅜-in. rubber bushing. In wiring the lamp, the cord should enter thru the bushing from the outside, and under and up thru the pipe to the socket. The drawing for the pipe is shown at Figure 85, also a bushing which is brazed into the top of the pipe and threaded for a ⅛-in. pipe. The ⅛-in. steam pipe and bushing are shown in position in the illustration at one end of the pipe. This small pipe is for the lamp socket to be screwed onto. The other end of the large pipe is to be threaded and screwed into the base. The pipe should be screwed into the base far enough, so that the threads will not be exposed to the outside and the surplus cut off. The pipe when screwed tight should be brazed to the base. In doing this, the borax and spelter should be applied to the under side, after the base is well heated, as the brass will discolor the iron on the top side. When the pipe is brazed it should be made to stand vertical.

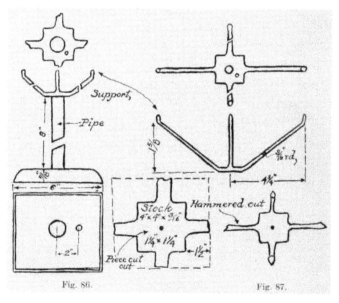

Fig. 86. Fig. 87.

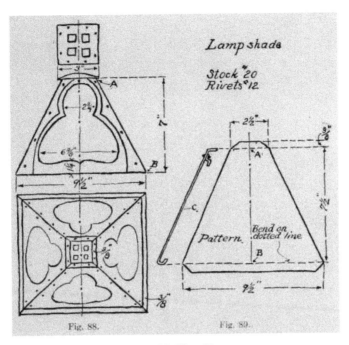

Fig. 88. Fig. 89.

In Figure 86 is shown the lamp standard with the shade support in position. The support has a hole in the center to fit the ⅛-in. steam pipe at the top of the standard. When the support is in place another ⅛-in. hole is drilled thru it into the pipe. A pin is driven into the hole so that the support cannot be moved around. The lamp socket when screwed down makes the support tight. In making the support the center part is cut from a plate ³⁄₁₆ in. by 4 by 4 in. and ³⁄₁₆ in. round soft steel bars are welded on for the arms. In Figure 87 is shown the drawing which does not need explanation. The drawing for the pattern is shown at Figure 88 and the pattern for one section at Figure 89. In developing the pattern which is very simple the top drawing, Figure 88, represents the shade which should be drawn full size. The length from A to B is then laid off on the center line of the pattern, which in this case measures 7½ in. The top and bottom of shade shows a return of ⅜ in. which should be added to the length of the pattern. The width of the top and bottom of the shade is then drawn, also diagonal lines which will complete the pattern. The edge view of the pattern is shown at C. The ⅜-in. bend at the top is made so that the cap can be riveted on. The one at the bottom is to receive the glass. This was explained on a previous page in describing the making of a hall lantern. In assembling the shade, corner angles are used to fasten the sections together, which was also explained for the hall lantern. The top cap is put on last and fastened with rivets.

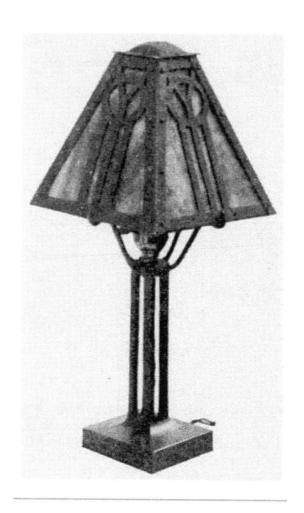